HOW
TO THINK
LIKE A GREAT
GRAPHIC
DESIGNER

DEBBIE MILLMAN

WITH A FOREWORD BY STEVEN HELLER

ALLWORTH PRESS
NEW YORK

School of
VISUAL ARTS

ALLWORTH PRESS BOOKS MAY BE PURCHASED IN BULK AT SPECIAL DIS-
COUNTS FOR SALES PROMOTION, CORPORATE GIFTS, FUND-RAISING, OR
EDUCATIONAL PURPOSES. SPECIAL EDITIONS CAN ALSO BE CREATED TO
SPECIFICATIONS. FOR DETAILS, CONTACT THE SPECIAL SALES DEPART-
MENT, ALLWORTH PRESS, 307 WEST 36TH STREET, 11TH FLOOR, NEW
YORK, NY 10018 OR INFO@SKYHORSEPUBLISHING.COM.

18 17 16   6 5 4

PUBLISHED BY ALLWORTH PRESS, AN IMPRINT OF SKYHORSE PUBLISH-
ING, INC.307 WEST 36TH STREET, 11TH FLOOR, NEW YORK, NY 10018.

ALLWORTH PRESS® IS A REGISTERED TRADEMARK OF SKYHORSE PUB-
LISHING, INC.®, A DELAWARE CORPORATION.

WWW.ALLWORTH.COM

COVER DESIGN BY RODRIGO CORRAL
INTERIOR DESIGN BY RODRIGO CORRAL DESIGN
EDITED BY JEREMY LEHRER
AUTHOR PHOTOGRAPH BY MARYANNERUSSELL.COM

LIBRARY OF CONGRESS CATALOGING-IN-PUBLICATION DATA

MILLMAN, DEBBIE.
    HOW TO THINK LIKE A GREAT GRAPHIC DESIGNER / DEBBIE MILLMAN.
        P. CM.
    INCLUDES INDEX.
    ISBN-13: 978-1-58115-496-2 (PBK.)
    ISBN-10: 1-58115-496-8 (PBK.)
    1. GRAPHIC ARTS. 2. GRAPHIC ARTISTS—INTERVIEWS. I. TITLE.
    NC1000.M55 2007
    741.6—DC22

                        2007029826

For a great man:
My father, Martin Millman

Contents

ix   *Foreword by* STEVEN HELLER

1   *Introduction by* DEBBIE MILLMAN

5   MICHAEL BIERUT
*"What actually drove me to a therapist was that I had
a very unhealthy obsession with laundry."*

19   CARIN GOLDBERG
*"When I was growing up, designers were anonymous.
They didn't do schtick."*

29   MILTON GLASER
*"At the end of the day, I would pound them into oblivion and
look forward to the next day when I could recreate the world."*

41   PAULA SCHER
*"I wanted to make wonderful things, things that other
people liked, things that were important and mattered."*

53   STEFAN SAGMEISTER
"A famous designer is like a famous electrician."

67   NEVILLE BRODY
*"It was time to take stock, check my shoes, buy nice clothes,
live comfortably for a while, and see the world again."*

77   PETER SAVILLE
*"The sort of weird realization I got at Pentagram—once
I was in—was that they really wanted me to recant and
see that they were the one true church."*

93   EMILY OBERMAN & BONNIE SIEGLER/
NUMBER 17
*"We should have answered each other's questions, because
I knew your answer, and I'm sure that you know mine."*

103   JAMES VICTORE
"I try to approach everything as a 'god job.'"

115   JOHN MAEDA
"The same sensitivity you can have with an A4 sheet does not apply to people."

125   PAUL SAHRE
"I thought I was going to make my fortune being like Charles Schulz."

135   CHIP KIDD
"Those are the closest moments to sex in graphic design."

145   JESSICA HELFAND
"I'm too obtuse one day, too vapid the next. Too abstract and intellectual. Too cultivated. Not cultivated enough."

155   SEYMOUR CHWAST
"After my mind has done its job, Mr. Hand takes over."

161   LUCILLE TENAZAS
"I would tell myself that I was not going to be embarrassed calling someone for the third time in a month."

173   VAUGHAN OLIVER
"I would like to get back my love for graphic design, because I think I've lost it."

183   STEFF GEISSBUHLER
"I certainly danced a few rounds with the devil in my career, and he often took the lead."

191   STEPHEN DOYLE
"At that moment, I felt that Milton Glaser was on par with William Shakespeare and Julius Caesar."

203   ABBOTT MILLER
"Am I too concerned with conventional notions of beauty and good taste?"

213   MASSIMO VIGNELLI
"Love is a cake that comes in layers."

227   *Acknowledgments*

229   *About the Author*

231   *Index*

Foreword
by Steven Heller

It is not true that the interviewer is only as good
as the interviewee. While a generous and articulate guest is key to any scintillating exchange, the
interviewer cannot be passive, laconic, or, worse,
uninformed. Interviews must be tackled with zeal,
and the interviewer must control the discussion
while waiting for that unexpected revelation to eke
out. A skilled host must therefore prepare exhaus-
tively: Take James Lipton of "Inside the Actors
Studio," with his famously large stack of blue index
cards, each containing a pointed question neatly
integrated into a systematic progression; while he
theatrically examines the narratives of his subjects'
careers, he is always flexible enough to flow with
unforeseen currents of conversation. Lipton builds
on surprising admissions while keeping the interview on track. And this is no mean feat.

Interviewing requires considerable acumen
to enable both the expressive and, especially, the
reticent guest to open up. The worst-case scenario,
the monosyllabic subject who resolutely guards
each pearl of thought or emotion, can be avoided
with a battery of insightful queries that forces a
kind of challenge—in the good sense.

Debbie Millman, who has hosted the Internet radio program "Design Matters" since 2005,
always does her homework—and then some. With
her dulcet intonations, she plies each of her visitors
with questions designed to evoke the unexpected

response. At the same time, she inspires their confidence, owing to her sincere interest in the life and work she's exploring. Her style is certainly not of the "gotcha," Barbara Walters variety, yet neither does she wear kid gloves. I've been interviewed by her on several occasions, and each time, her approach is somewhat different, tailored to the moment. Friendly yet challenging, she proceeds smoothly from the initial introductions to more free-form conversation. Debbie comes to the discussion well-prepared, not with cursory cheat sheets, but pages of incisive talking points garnered from extensive research.

Though she is the host of the only radio show devoted in large part to graphic design, Debbie was not trained as a journalist. The first time I saw her name was a few years ago on the then-fledgling design blog Speak Up, where she duked it out with founder Armin Vit about brands (which had become one of the forum's *bêtes noires*). Debbie's parries and thrusts with the critically skeptical Vit and his cohorts on the efficacy of branding made for a compelling debate, and her arguments were persuasive and eminently logical. But why shouldn't she be convincing? Debbie is a partner at Sterling Brands, a New York–based brand identity firm, where her eloquence is well-utilized. She's gracefully made it to the top of a male-dominated business, and her considerable strategic marketing savvy allows her to be an effective advocate of design.

In large part, this is because she is a devoted aficionado of design and designers, although her interests extend into realms of science and psychology (which she poetically examines in her own blog, *http://debbiemillman.blogspot.com*). Perhaps another reason she is so adept in conversation is that she truly enjoys learning from others. Her passionate concern for the practice and history of design makes her interviews captivating, though listening to designers talk about their craft could potentially be too arcane even for those in the field. Yet Debbie makes her program riveting by balancing, for instance, the real skinny on Michael Bierut's obsessive tendencies with insights about his design for Saks Fifth Avenue's shopping bag.

I often paraphrase Paul Rand's statement about how he intuitively came up with an idea and then found the rationale for it later, which isn't to say that comprehending the roots of a concept, or even learning about the technology behind it, is bad, but it takes oratory skill and an understanding of nuance to deconstruct a project so that the details are not banal. The virtue of interviews with designers—as opposed to prose narratives about them—is that they cut through the intellectualizing and get to the creative essence, whatever that might be.

While an interview is not inherently easy, the best enable the voice—the intelligence, humor, irony, even sarcasm—of the designer to emerge. Debbie has, through her tête-à-têtes with the designers in this book, managed to extract the nitty-gritty of their practices without sacrificing their respective humanity. She allows them to speak, but never too much—or too little.

Introduction
by Debbie Millman

From: Steff Geissbuhler
Date: December 3, 2006 6:10:45 PM EST
To: Debbie Millman
Subject: Re: How To Think Like A Great Graphic Designer

Debbie,

I think that we talk to ourselves, about ourselves, way too much. We have conferences where we talk to ourselves, we give each other awards, we publish each other's work and words, and basically we pat each other on our backs.

I'm afraid that your book will be read by Graphic Designers only and therefore simply add to the incestuous writing in our profession. However, I found myself answering your questions to see how I would respond. I might be cringing when it's published, but here it is.

I hope you don't mind my critical point of view.

I often get questions like this from students, and whenever I do, I get the sense that they are fishing for a recipe to become a successful designer.

With best regards,

Steff

Steff Geissbuhler, Partner
C&G Partners

Despite its title, this book will not provide the reader with a recipe to think like some of the most accomplished graphic designers of our time. Consider it instead a glimpse into the minds of these revered masters, in order to understand the way they think and why.

This book didn't start out quite this way. Initially, I set out to create an anthology that did, in fact, attempt to uncover common denominators and describe the thought processes of those venerated in the design field. Many of my original questions smacked of superficiality, and even though I was miffed when I first received Steff Geissbuhler's reply, I quickly came to my senses. After all, Steff had a point. Perhaps we *do* talk to ourselves, about ourselves, way too much. But given the fact that design is a fairly young field, is there anything inherently wrong with a robust internal dialogue?

Identifying what constitutes a great mind, whether logical or magical or whimsical, is a necessarily subjective endeavor. Emulating a great mind is an even more complex proposition. There is no objective way to be great, let alone recommend an audience-tested, foolproof way to create with elegance, ambition, and artistry. If I was going to add to the discourse of an already cacophonous environment, I wanted to go beyond tactical quantifications of how designers work. Instead, I set out to engage in deeply psychological discussions in order to understand what motivates these practitioners to think and behave in the unique manner that they do.

Design invests raw matter with what Bruce Mau calls "performativity"—it endows an inert material with a capacity to incite action. But in order to accomplish this most effectively, designers must conjure this power. *This* process is complicated. The fundamental backbone of any good design solution is measured not only by what motivates an audience to think in a particular way, but what inspires them to *feel* a response.

Design is one of the few disciplines that is a science as well as an art. Effective, meaningful design requires intellectual, rational rigor along with the ability to elicit emotions and beliefs. Thus, designers must balance both the logic and lyricism of humanity every time they design something, a task that requires a singularly mysterious skill.

Many of the designers interviewed in this book describe design as a problem-solving activity, yet it's clear that these designers do far more than that. Despite the obvious similarities, there is one trait shared by each and every person in this group of designers: high levels of empathy. Their sensitivity has given them the ability to logically, poetically, and telegraphically transfer ideas from one mind to another. It imbues the talented designer with a wizardry of sorts, an uncanny ability to create a message and a purity of expression that cuts through the modern-day chaos of sensory overload.

This is the remarkable power every designer featured in this book has in abundance. In my interview with him, Milton Glaser observed, "You convey your ideas by the authenticity of your being." Throughout these pages, there are a great many masters who offer ideas and wisdom through their authenticity. Ultimately, the conversations contained in this book reveal how designers think and view the world, but they are also a testament to how and why great designers are able to create the extraordinary work that they do.

Michael Bierut

When I first contacted Michael Bierut about talking with him for this book, he asked that we conduct the interview via e-mail. When I received his responses, I found it hard to believe that Bierut—coeditor of the anthology Looking Closer: Critical Writings on Graphic Design *and a cofounder of the blog* Design Observer*—could possibly have written what were easily the most uninteresting answers I had received thus far. Two examples:*

> *What was your first creative memory?*
> I'm not sure I have any creative memories.

> *Did you ever have serious aspirations to pursue any other type of career, and if so, what?*
> No.

Yet Michael, a Pentagram partner since 1990, is one of the most important and acclaimed designers working today. Not only has he won hundreds of design awards, not only is his work represented in the permanent collection of the Museum of Modern Art, but Michael is charming, engaging, witty, and brilliant. The interview contained none of these attributes.

I was despondent: The idea of not including Bierut in a book about esteemed contemporary designers was unthinkable. After some nudging, he agreed to an in-person interview. He graciously gave me two hours of his time, and our discussion ended up being one of the funniest and most entertaining interviews I conducted for the book.

How would you say that you and your fellow
Pentagram partner Paula Scher are different?

Paula says what she thinks. I admire her a lot for that. I have given up wishing that I could be like that. I've discovered I'm really averse to conflict. I think I was brought up to be too polite! The negative aspect of this is that I'm passive-aggressive. I have deeply rooted neuroses and flaws, which actually compel me to fix things so that as many people as possible—actually everyone in the world—likes me.

You don't seem to have an unhappy bone in your body.

That could also be denial. Paula used to say that I was the kind of guy who could be like this for 30 years, and then one day come into the office with a machine gun and go postal. But I think I've gotten over that, also. On the other hand, as you can see in the case of a politician desperate for everyone's approval, you end up getting really confused about what your own convictions are.

In terms of design, I really admire and envy designers who always must do it their way and can walk away from a job if it's not done on their own terms. I remember early on in my career, I worked with a guy who was absolutely secure in his convictions; though he liked it when people agreed with him, it wasn't necessary in order for him to feel that he was right. Whereas if I go into a client meeting, and I can't sell something, I feel like I've failed and my convictions get shaken.

When I first started talking directly to clients, I had some moments where I got so obsessed with obtaining approval about a project that I mistook that for doing the job right. By the time one project was about to go to press, I remember my boss—Massimo Vignelli—saying to me, "What is this?" And I said, "This is a job for so-and-so." And he said, "Why does it look this way?" And I started to say, "Well, they did this, and then they did that, and it had to be this," and he said, "No. This is awful. We can't let this go." He picked up the phone at my desk and called up the boss of the boss of the boss of the guy who had been jerking me around for three weeks and said, "You know this thing you're doing for the blah blah blah? I'm not sure it's quite right. I want to do it right. We'll send it over after we do one more thing to it. We have time, right?" Then he sat there and scraped off all the shit that had accrued on it over the past three weeks and did something crisp and right and perfect.

Massimo had this saying: "Once a work is out there, it doesn't really matter what the excuses were."

It doesn't matter if you didn't have enough time or if the client was an idiot. The only thing that counts is what you've designed, and whether it's good or bad.

These are words to live by. I have overcompensated by trying to do lots and lots of work in the hopes that something good will get out there. I think my batting percentage is so low that I just have to get lots of at-bats in order to even the score at all.

Do you really believe that?

Yes. I like working fast, and though now I'm old enough to know better, I've gotten addicted to "closing my eyes and shooting." It's a bad way to hit a target, actually.

Well, if you had missed the target a number of times, you probably would have stopped working that way. The fact that you haven't stopped means you've had some success.

Yes. Sometimes if you're fast, it's mistaken for genius. But I don't think it's necessarily good. You can get acclimated to a certain way of working; you get some useful habits, but you also pick up others that aren't very good.

There are times when I know that I have
to write something for Design Observer [the blog
about design and visual culture founded by Bierut,
Jessica Helfand, William Drenttel, and Rick
Poynor], and I'll keep reminding myself that I have
to post it on Thursday, and yet I'll keep putting it
off and putting it off. As long as I know what the
subject is, and as long as I've been thinking about it
for a week or so, when I'm ready, I can start writing
and continue onward all the way to the end—one
paragraph after another until it's finished. It's as if
I'm working with an outline that was written down
to my elbow. While it might seem that I haven't been
working all that time, I actually have—it was just
unconscious or "sub-conscious" working.

You were germinating.

When I first started writing, one of the reasons I
liked it so much was because it was so hard to do.
I would finish a piece I had written and go back and
look at it and reread it again, and I'd think, "Wow
this really is great, it's really nice the way I did this."
It reminded me of the way I felt about design in the
very beginning. I remember looking at the first
prototype I designed. I just couldn't take my eyes
off of it; it was so beautiful, so real, and so perfect.
But over enough time, it becomes all too flawed,
or worse, you become bored with it.

Likewise the first time you receive a finished
piece; I've got my first printed piece somewhere in
my basement. I've got samples of all sorts of things:
a brochure for a lamp company that I did 25 years
ago. It was a two-color piece, and I think I have
20 copies of it. At the time, I thought it was really
important, and I had to have that many copies of
it because it was just so beautiful. And of course it
wasn't that good, but it was one of the first things
I designed that got printed. I was mesmerized by
the realness of it. It had me all agog.

I think really brilliant people do a number of different things when they're working. They're able to force themselves to put a lot of time into things and give them a lot of attention, and not succumb to the shortcuts that regular practice can lead to. Stefan Sagmeister works like this. Or else you have someone like Tibor Kalman, who purposely fixed it so that he didn't repeat himself.

How did he do that?

He would do two things. One, he'd be very ambitious about doing things in a new genre. If someone came to him to design a brochure for a museum exhibition, and he'd already designed a brochure for a museum exhibition, he'd say, "No, I want to design *the exhibition*," even though he'd never designed an exhibition before.

He also—and I think this was a kind of pathology/genius—he was able to burn his bridges behind him so he could ensure he wouldn't repeat himself. After he did the animated "Nothing But Flowers" video for the Talking Heads, he received a lot of calls from television directors. They would say, "Hey Tibor, could you do that typography thing on my commercial, could you do this, could you do that?"

Tibor hated being hired because someone thought he knew how to do something well. I love being hired for it. I have an unrestrained enthusiasm for being hired to do something that I do well. It can get to be tough when you've done something over and over again, especially if it's a genre of work that you have a reputation for and you keep getting calls to do another one and then another one. Eventually, you run out of ways to do it differently, and you find that it's hard to disguise the fact that this very thing that has given you so much pleasure is now not enough.

It's a basic psychological reaction; it's like rats with pellets in a maze. You know exactly what gave you pleasure the first time you tried it, and you try to keep repeating the thing that led to that success. And just like any addict, you know the subsequent payback is insufficient. You remember that the first time it happened, it was wonderful; and by the tenth time, it's, "Ho hum, here's another one. I'm not even going to take a picture of it, never mind 20 copies in the basement."

Are you addicted to anything?
Reading.

Reading? You consider reading an addiction?
I have a real fear of being alone with nothing to read. Of being on a plane with nothing to read. I take it to an extreme. There's something really extreme about going to an amusement park with my kids and needing to take a book with me just in case the line for rides is too long. I think a lot of it is to inoculate myself, to keep my mind full so that I don't have any time for self-reflection. I've really tried to improve this.

Do you think that you're trying to distract yourself, trying not to confront something?
I think on some level, yes. But I think on the other hand, it's just like a lot of compulsions: I also have to jog three miles every morning.

What happens if you don't?
Well. You really want to know? I have a chart in my basement, and I have years and years of calendars on clipboards. They all have different markings on different days. There are markings I make when I do certain things, and certain marks I make when I do other things. Sometimes I give myself a special dispensation not to run, which is either one of three reasons: Either I have an 8:30 A.M. appointment, it's raining pretty hard, or it's below ten degrees—not including the windchill,

but the actual thermometer reading. For these reasons, I'm allowed not to run that morning. No one else cares. Literally, no one else cares.

Why did you choose ten degrees as the cutoff point?

It's single digits. It's really cold when it's nine degrees, even when you're running. Twelve degrees you can run—it's not so bad. Less than nine degrees, running becomes unbearable.

If I sleep late, I draw a little sad face for that day on the calendar, a frown face. If I don't run, I'll make an *X*. It's horrible, all these really compulsive things. On the other hand, exercise is good for you.

So this calendar is sort of a hieroglyphic diary of your life.

Yes, it is. But it's nothing I'm proud of. I think it's fucked-up and embarrassing, to tell you the truth. It is not worth emulating at all. Oh, and there's more. I keep notebooks. I have 79 of them. They go back to 1982. They're all unlined, which is really hard to find, harder to find now than ever.

Do you have boxes of these notebooks stockpiled?

New ones? I'm about to run out. I had someone score me a whole cache about two years ago. I can find the genesis of every single thing I've ever worked on in them. And then there are a lot of notes from meetings and lots and lots of phone numbers.

How many do you carry around at a time?

I carry the current one and the previous one.

When you're first carrying around numbers 79 and 80, how does it feel to put number 78 away?

I honestly can't say there's that much ceremony involved. The only thing I can say for sure is that there are two that I've lost. I remember both of them very distinctly. One of them I had just started, and I lost it, so I simply restarted it. The other one was almost completed, and I left it in a bathroom in Heathrow Airport.

Now, you may ask, "Why was it in the bathroom in Heathrow Airport?" Well, I was sitting on the can. I had nothing else to read. I didn't have a book, I didn't have a newspaper, and I didn't have a magazine. That's my nightmare: trying to go to the bathroom with nothing to read. So I took out my notebook and started looking at it, and then I finished and washed my hands and went away whistling. I forget when I realized that it was gone. It's interesting in that I found I could survive quite well without it.

Sometimes, I'll go to a meeting and forget my notebook, so I can't write things down. When I'm working on a project, I'll have a meeting with clients and ask lots of questions and take lots of notes, all with the idea that I'm going to be poring over them at great length later. But I really don't, because it's already in my mind. Sometimes, I'll go back to check to see, "What were those three things they said?" I think just the act of writing something down helps clarify things in your mind.

Right now, I'm moving my desk at Pentagram because the available seat for Luke Hayman—who joined Pentagram as a partner—is right on the end. It would be rude to put the new guy on the end. So I'm going to sit at that desk, which means that I have to move all of my stuff. My stuff includes all those notebooks, all 77 of them. And I have a bunch of calendars I used before I went digital. Every once in a while, I'll open up one from 1991 and look at all the names and appointments and things that, at the time, seemed so important. Meetings that I was really worried about, things that I was getting calls four times a day about, and I wonder, "Where did it all go? Where are they now?" It's so strange, everything has disappeared. The only thing that stays behind is the work.

I think I keep things I've worked on around me as evidence that I've participated in something, though they do become useful when you're the victim of a random IRS audit.

Yes. I've often said that if I'm ever the victim of a random audit, I'm just going to kill myself. And people say, "Why? You haven't done anything wrong." And I say, "I have done wrong. I don't know what I've done wrong, but I've done lots of things wrong. I don't know what they are. But I am so guilty."

What frustrates you?

Physical things, stupid things. I'll get really mad at a drawer that won't close properly. I bang it shut over and over again while shouting, "This motherfucking thing just won't stay closed!" Now that I'm aware of this, I'm much better at it, actually. I had a period in my life when I had anger issues.

What about your wife, did she ever see it?

Oh yes, she would see it. But I wouldn't get mad at her. I would get mad at anyone who wouldn't hang up their coats. I would get obsessed with neatness issues. What actually drove me to a therapist was that I had a very unhealthy obsession with laundry. I'm in charge of doing the laundry in my family— and I've gone from simply doing the laundry to having an entire weekend-long methodology for doing the laundry.

Without going into too much detail, it had to do with what order things were washed in, and most importantly, how the clothes are folded and stacked. Now, keep in mind that five people live in my house. I got to a point where I would fold my son's pants in a certain way. All of the jeans would be together, the khakis would all be together, and the shirts would be organized in a certain way.

He has three basic kinds of shirts: short-sleeved polo T-shirts, short-sleeved shirts, and long-sleeved shirts. So they would have to be organized like this: collared polo shirts first, then long-sleeved shirts, then short-sleeved T-shirts. And I would do this over and over again for all five people in the house. Actually getting all of this staged properly takes a lot of time.

What made me mad was that no one seemed to appreciate my efforts. They would demonstrate their lack of appreciation by just grabbing any goddamn thing they wanted right out of the pile. And the pile would topple over. Yet, while someone might think I had a legitimate cause for irritation, it turns out this whole thing was really an attempt to attain some sort of control.

Did it give you great joy to see those stacks of neatly folded clothing?

Sure. Do you like to cook? I hate to cook. I'll tell you why: You get it all ready and people just mess it up. I like to wash the dishes. You get them washed and then they're neatly organized, perfectly clean— sometimes they're clean for weeks.

Are there any areas in your life where you're messy?

Unfortunately, not anymore. I wasn't like this as a kid. Well, my desk is a little messy. My books are messy.

It's funny; I'm a fairly messy designer. It doesn't show in my work, but my process is messy.

Sometimes someone will ask, "Oh, we're doing a piece about process, can you show us your design process?" And I know exactly what they want. They want this sequence of rough sketches leading to almost-rough sketches leading to almost-finished work leading to the final, chosen piece.

I don't have those things; I don't work in a sort of methodical way. A lot of your questions are about creativity, and I don't think design involves that much creativity. It involves creativity in the way doing a crossword puzzle involves creativity.

You need some imagination and knowledge. I think of artists as creative because they have to invent something out of nothing. I think designers design because they can't invent something out of nothing. Or at least that's why I design.

So you see design as more of an exercise in connectivity rather than creativity?

Yes. One of the things I admire is seeing a designer re-purposing something rather than inventing something brand-new. I remember when I first saw the 1990 Time Warner annual report that Kent Hunter did—the "Why?" Annual. There wasn't a single thing in it that was new. It was all ripped out of old *Spy* magazines. But there was something about the audacity of it. Being able to put all those things together for this particular purpose was amazing. But if you actually examined it, there wasn't much original form-making. Other people had done the original form-making.

A lot of it was taken from Rick Valicenti, who is very compelled to make things. He can start with a blank piece of paper. His forms seem to come intuitively, and his clients align themselves with his interest in making these things, and they get the benefit of it.

When I get a request to come up with something brand-new, it's really hard for me. Really hard. I end up having to invent a problem in order to do it. And that is something I just love doing. It gives me great physical pleasure to solve problems. I remember watching Massimo Vignelli do things over and over again. But each time, they were always slightly different. He found enormous pleasure in finding slightly different ways of doing the thing that he loved to do.

And good designers can't always do that. They are who they are, and somehow as their work develops—no matter how eclectic they think they are—they end up finding that there's a certain handiwork that comes out of them that is just as compulsive as a lot of the compulsions that we all—some of us at least—are driven by.

Given your self-admitted sense of being deeply flawed, to what do you attribute your success and popularity?

I remember being in high school. This was before I took the SATs, and I wanted to prepare for them. This was back in the '70s, and there were no SAT preparatory classes. I remember someone saying, "You can't study for these tests. It's natural." I remember thinking, "Can't study? Excellent! In that case, let me not study." I remember I carried two new Number 2 pencils, and I showed up on time and I sat down and took the tests.

And I got very good SAT scores. I remember my guidance counselor telling me they were so good that I could get a scholarship and go to an Ivy League school with my scores. And I remember thinking that I was good at art. I already knew what graphic design was. My guidance counselor thought I was really smart and felt it was a waste for me to go into art instead of becoming a doctor or a lawyer. I thought that there must be a lot of smart doctors and lawyers but I didn't think there could be quite as many smart commercial artists. And I remember thinking, "I bet a smart commercial artist would really have an edge on things."

And that's what I think I am. I'm a smart commercial artist. There were at least two other kids in my college classes that were better natural designers than I was. But at the end of the day, having something issue forth from just your imagination will only get you so far.

That doesn't win you a project. That doesn't find a specific solution to allow you to indulge your creativity, that doesn't help you explain that solution to your clients, that doesn't help you do all the

HOW TO THINK LIKE A GREAT GRAPHIC DESIGNER

hard work that will muster up big groups of people to do major things.

All of those things take something else: brains. I actually think that I've compensated for whatever flaws and shortcomings I have as a creative person by being smart and well-read and by working really, really hard. And by getting more at-bats. I seem to hit a lot of home runs because I have ten times as many at-bats as everyone else in the league. Meanwhile, the stands are littered with foul balls and strikeouts. And no one knows about them because I don't count those. Right?

Carin Goldberg

It was the summer of 1983. David Bowie, The Police, and Evelyn "Champagne" King filled the airwaves. When a little-known artist burst onto the scene, the way our culture viewed celebrity and the cult of visual reinvention was changed forever.

I am, of course, alluding to Madonna. The moment I saw her first album, I knew something was forever different. I am not, however, referring to the singer herself. I am describing the profound impact of the album cover. Unapologetically in-your-face, the cover was charismatically smart and sassy. But here's the kicker: The cover conveyed an attitude that was distinctly Madonna long before the singer had cultivated her characteristic bravado. And that cover (and the necklace that graced Madonna in the photograph) was created by Carin Goldberg.

Carin has been working in the field of graphic design for over 30 years, completing design and advertising commissions for major publishing, music, and TV corporations. She's headed her own firm, Carin Goldberg Design, since 1982. She designed and authored her first book, titled Catalog, *in 2001, and has been working on* Home, *a second collection.*

Carin and I talked over lunch at a Manhattan eatery and lingered until the restaurant began to serve dinner. We discussed career relevance and longevity, her dispute with Tibor Kalman, the importance of taking risks, her longtime friendship with Paula Scher, and, of course, fishing for flounder.

What do you love most about design?

There is something very gratifying when you're involved in your work—once you've hit that point of focus and you're really in it. That's what we all look for. We all wait for that moment when we're in it, and we love the making of the piece.

What don't you like?

The schtick.

The schtick?

A lot of design has become about schtick. People might take me to task for this, but you know what it reminds me of? It's like this: Someone starts off in life very beautiful. Then there's someone else who's not so beautiful. But in the end, both people get wrinkled and old. We're all on the same planet, and it really doesn't matter. The real dilemma is this: Should we just grab the schtick while we can, and use it? Because when we hit our fifties or sixties, we'll all be in the same boat.

It's really hard nowadays to maintain a career in graphics, particularly in the field of graphic design. It's a youth-oriented business. I often wonder about whether I'm relevant or not. But that's not how I was brought up. It's not what I saw.

When I was growing up, designers were anonymous. They weren't celebrities. They did not write books. They didn't do schtick. Not one of them.

So it became clear to me at a certain point in my career that being publicly clever might be the only thing that could give my career any kind of longevity. It has been a rough thing to come to grips with. I'm certainly not a shrinking violet, but I don't get great enjoyment out of getting up there publicly and doing that kind of thing. I'd rather do the work. I also think that a lot of people find that when the schtick really works, they're on planes half the time doing the schtick.

I wonder when they have the time to do the work, and I'm also suspicious as to whether they actually have "the work."

You've had a long and illustrious career. How would you describe it?

I'll tell you a story. When I was little, I used to go fishing with my father. He was an outdoorsman, and we used to go out to the Long Island Sound in a little boat. We'd put our rods out, and we would hope that we would hit big pockets of flounder. And sometimes you would hit them, and sometimes you wouldn't. But sometimes if we hit that hole, we could fill two giant galvanized cans with flounder, and we would bring all of the flounder home to the neighbors. Everyone would wait for us to come back, and then they knew they'd be eating flounder for the entire winter.

And that's how I think of my career. I hit some flounder holes. I hit the record business at a time when flounders were there for me. I hit the book business at a time when flounders were there for me. My colleagues and I were under the radar, spinning up these flounders, and I remember thinking, "Is anybody watching this, why aren't they with us getting the flounders, too?" We could not believe we were alone in this great discovery.

That was what it was like for me. I was very lucky to find these flounder holes, these moments of utter fertility. I was lucky. Lucky to be there, while it was all happening. But after the luck, there was all the hard work. That's the part that makes me just absolutely livid, when I hear men talking about women and their careers. In my own career, I had to be as tenacious as a dog with a bone.

I made sure I was observing and watching and looking over the shoulders of the right people and learning from them and killing myself to learn everything I could. So my career has been about luck and hard work.

*Having projects come your way might be luck but
doing a good job with them is much more than that.
Let's talk about security. How important has security
been to you?*

I remember the moment in 1983 when I knew I
would never be a painter. It was because I would
never survive. I've given lectures on this. I open
it up by saying, "I'm a graphic designer because I
like nice sheets and towels." And I realize too that
I don't like to be alone. Occasionally I do, but often
I don't. There is a small part of me that loves being
solitary. As a kid, I used to run away to be by myself
and draw. That's how it all started.

**As a graphic designer, I like collab-
oration. I don't want to be in a cold garret somewhere
smoking unfiltered Camels all by myself with paint all
over my body—because I like sheets too much.**

Speaking of compromise, I remember for
my first job at CBS Records, I hired Milton Glaser
to do an illustration for a Carole King ad. As I was
dialing his phone number, I was shaking in my
boots. It was like calling the pope. I remember I
rang him up, and I asked him to do an illustration
for a full-page ad for Carole King. He sent me an
illustration that was—well, let's say it wasn't his
best. I knew it. Even at that age, I knew it, even
though I thought of him as God's gift to the universe. So I called his rep and told him we were
hoping he'd give us something different.

Milton absolutely refused. He just said,
"Sorry, what you see is what you get." And I went
home and cried and didn't sleep for a week because
I thought I had offended Milton Glaser. It wasn't
until many years later that I realized that he had
done the right thing by standing up for what he
thought was right. If you don't, people will take
everything you have. You may risk losing a job,
but in the grand scheme of things, I believe that

by standing up for yourself, you're doing the graphic design business a service.

I used to get angry with friends of mine who were also doing book-jacket design as freelancers. They wouldn't charge for messenger bills and they wouldn't charge for mechanicals, and I'd say, "You know, you're fucking it up for the rest of us." And they'd say, "I'm afraid I won't get called again." And it just drove me crazy. I'm a big believer in the bungee jump. I think you have to do the right thing and the fair thing even if you're afraid.

When I stopped designing book jackets, it was a huge bungee jump. I knew I could have been shooting myself in the foot. But I couldn't get up in the morning anymore and go to my desk; I could not deal with the people I was dealing with anymore. It was over. And I think you have to take those risks. It takes awhile to recover, but in the end, you end up ahead of the game. Morally and emotionally, you've evolved.

Back in 1989, Tibor Kalman said that you and Paula Scher and Louise Fili were pillaging design history. Why do you think he felt that way?

In some ways, what he said was valid. In retrospect, I can't really fault him for what he was saying. It was a time when we were changing things. Changing the way design was being done. If you look at what I was doing, what Paula Scher was doing, and what Louise Fili was doing, it had to happen. Design was evolving. If you look at the architecture of that time, if you look at photography, it was all happening at once. There was a discovery of something that we had previously not known about. It was inexplicable. You can call it postmodernism, for lack of a better description. My husband, Jim Biber, went through it in architecture. It's the nature of the way these movements occur. All of a sudden, there were books around that hadn't been there before. Suddenly, we didn't want to be art directors

anymore. We didn't want to shoot a picture of somebody and stick a name on the cover. We wanted to
design things.

So how did that make you a pillager of design history
rather than, say, a catalyst for change?

Paula got crucified for her Swatch watch campaign
because it was an homage to Herbert Bayer. My
book cover for James Joyce's *Ulysses* got killed
because it was an homage to modernist posters.
I was asked to do something that was purely
typographic because the famous 1960s cover by
E. McKnight Kauffer was a big *U*. The publishers
didn't want to lose that tradition, and they wanted
me to do yet another big *U*, so I did 12 big *U*'s, and it
just so happened that the *U* they ended up with was
influenced by a Swiss design I had seen while doing
my research.

Now, if you think about it, there is no content in a *U*. The publishers did not want content.
I wanted content. They did not want me to read
Ulysses and then come up with a content-oriented
cover. Today, if you don't have content in some way
embedded in your jacket design, you are considered
to not be doing your job.

The same thing happened to me while designing the Oliver Sacks book, *The Man Who Mistook
His Wife for a Hat*. The publishers, in no uncertain
terms, didn't want me to do anything that was intellectual. I wanted to do something very surrealistic,
very Magritte; I wanted to go crazy. But I couldn't.
Now I've got this cover out there, and once it's out
there, it becomes fodder for people who are in a
position to denounce what you're doing, by criticiz-
ing you as part of a group or as an individual.

If you're doing a cover for the poetry of Rainer
Maria Rilke, you are essentially dealing with work
that can't change. The poetry itself is a work of art.
You investigate it as a work of art coming out of
a particular time. You ask: Who was Rilke? What

did the work look like then? How do you make it relevant? It's not like the "new and improved" Rilke. It's still Rilke. How can you visually educate your public? The publishers are reissuing this Rilke, it's not being rewritten. It's not like Dave Eggers is rewriting Rilke.

So what do you do? Do you do some modern, weird, wacky thing? No, you go to the source, because you want to maintain the work's integrity. At that time, in the 1980s, the general public was not aware of the Wienericht, and no one knew what the Bauhaus was. But 20 years later, this style has become ubiquitous. At the time, we were unearthing what had not yet been verbalized as a visual style.

Do you ever want to do anything besides graphic design?

Yes. I wanted to be a painter. I still would like to find a way that I can make my own work, perhaps painting or drawing. I still have a lot of ideas; I still feel like there's a side of me that would like to segue into this. I haven't figured out how to do it yet. I think this is because I'm still fundamentally excited about being a graphic designer.

Do you ever look back on your work and say, "Damn, that was a good cover design"?

It depends on the day. I might be proud of the fact I did it. I would likely be bored by it. I'd be bored because I would like another 15 years to do it all over. I did those book covers when I was pretty wet behind the ears. Now I feel I would have done some of it very differently. So I usually think, "Ugh, I would have done that differently…" I rarely think, "Oh, I was lucky I could do that, and that was kind of cool."

Every once in a while there are days when I might look at something and think, "Hmm, maybe that was a little ahead of the curve…" But it's up and down; it primarily has to do with wishing I didn't have to care about the body of work. I'm more interested in my next phase. Like anything you do in life, I'm proud of the fact that I've gotten better and that I have wisdom. I'm proud that I can impart that wisdom to my students, and that I can help myself grow and move on with that wisdom. That is very exciting to me. I can look back and say, "Wow, I've really learned a lot." But I'm not done yet.

How do you know when something you've designed is really good?

When you're having fun. "Fun" is a tricky word. People think that if you're having "fun," you're ignoring content, or you're ignoring the importance of the piece. But that's not true. I try to create visual imagery that is fun and funny and warm and artful, without being superficial, and work that has a point. I've always thought of myself—I mean, this is a dirty word, maybe there's a better word for it—but I have thought of myself as a populist on the one hand, and a complete elitist on the other hand.

There is a part of me that wants to speak a common language, and there is a part of me that wants to scramble the language.

I do have a consciousness about that. I don't have a manifesto that I've written about this, but I think that I have two very distinct takes on what my job is. I feel like I straddle the fence of the Abbott Miller, "What is the manifesto?" approach with Michael Bierut's "Dog Food" approach.

I don't think either can exist on its own. I think we must always try to elevate. It's the job we're supposed to be doing. We have to try to get people to feel comfortable—but not too comfortable. I don't like talking above people or making them feel that they have to work too hard to understand the design that's in front of them. I do want them to work, but I don't want to bore myself to death and make something uncomfortable either.

There's no question that I want there to be a voice in my work. Whether it's a conceit of something very simplistic or a conceit of ambiguity. I'm very clear about what I want to say. People have said—and sometimes they say it nicely and sometimes they say it with an agenda—that they see my work as being beautiful. For me, that has always been a prerequisite. I want my work to be beautiful. I want it to be smart, but I also want it to be beautiful. I don't have a lot of patience for "just smart," and sometimes I see work that is just smart—and it's not beautiful. Sometimes the typography isn't beautiful, and the craft isn't there. That drives me nuts. I think typography should be beautiful; otherwise, you should just be a writer.

I feel like there's so much more to be explored, but at the same time, I'm quite proud of what I have done. I get very emotional about the lucky trajectory of my career and the fact that I've been around such inspiring people. I could not have been more nourished. With all of its ups and downs, and strangeness, and shifts in expectations, and whatever it is that we all go through, I don't think I would have wanted to do anything any differently. I'm really proud of what I've done.

To be honest, before I knew you as well as I do now, I was intimidated by you.

It's so shocking because I think I am absolutely one of the most boundaryless people I know! I have very high expectations of myself, and I will tell you that I am very proud of who I am as a human being. I have no reservations about that. What you see is what you get, and I know that I have tremendous generosity of spirit. I can attribute that on some level to my mother; I can thank Paula Scher for helping to teach me things like that. I say this to you—and I'm not trying to sound humble—but it's beyond me that anyone would find me intimidating at all. I feel that if anything, I'm invisible most of the time.

Milton Glaser

Legendary. Brilliant. Intellectual. Sweetly naïve. These are just some of the qualities attributed over the years to Milton. I use his first name intentionally, but with no disrespect; as with John, Paul, Mick, or Keith, Milton's name is instantly recognizable.

And he is very much the superstar of graphic design. Yes, Mr. Glaser designed the Dylan poster and the I ♥ NY icon. Yes, his work as part of Push Pin, WBMG, New York magazine, and at his eponymous studio has meaningfully inspired generations of designers and pop-culture devotees. Yet while other great designers have created cool posters, beautiful book covers, and powerful logos, Milton Glaser has actually lifted this age he inhabits. Because of his integrity and his vision, he has enabled us all to walk on higher ground, and it is that for which we should be especially grateful.

Milton has often talked about the confusion many people have about the word "art." He has suggested that we replace the term with "work," and proposed the following maxim: "Work that goes beyond its functional intention and moves us in deep and mysterious ways we call great work."

Milton Glaser is a creator of great work. He is also a great man. What is so unique and precious is that he has achieved his stature honestly and authentically, without gimmicks, without hype, and without artifice. His work has a purity and an elegance that is timeless, profound, and dazzling.

My first question is one that I borrowed from you:
What's your first creative memory?

I don't know if I can identify the first. My memory
of the past is that there are so many areas that are
opaque, and I feel that there are so many areas that
I made up later in life.

Why is that?

Because retrieving the past is always treacherous.
The story of how I decided to become an artist is
this: When I was a very little boy, a cousin of mine
came to my house with a paper bag. He asked me
if I wanted to see a bird. I thought he had a bird in
the bag. He stuck his hand in the bag, and I realized
that he had drawn a bird on the side of a bag with a
pencil. I was astonished! I perceived this as being
miraculous. At that moment, I decided that was
what I was going to do with my life. Create miracles.

Why?

Because he had, out of pencil and paper, created a
living thing. And in my memory, it was well-drawn.
Up until that point in my life, I had never thought
about drawing anything other than what I could
illustrate symbolically: smoke, sun, tree. To actually
see something that looked like what it was and see
somebody in the act of making it convincingly—
that moment became identified with my decision
to make things. My life became about making things
and drawing things.

Here's another memory: I was eight years
old, and I had rheumatic fever. I was at home and
in bed for a year. In a certain sense, the only thing
that kept me alive was this: Every day, my mother
would bring me a wooden board and a pound of
modeling clay, and I would create a little universe
out of houses, tanks, warriors. At the end of the day,
I would pound them into oblivion and look forward
to the next day when I could recreate the world.

So I knew that my life was linked. My life and my psychology and my sense of self were linked to making things and the satisfaction that I derived from making things. The fact that I could maintain my attentiveness the whole day to making things was a very powerful stimulus in my life.

How did you feel at the end of the day when you dismantled your creation?

That was another great part. Dismantling it meant I would have another pound of clay to start again.

So there was no sorrow?

Quite the contrary. The pleasure was in making it and destroying it. I have never thought about this, but basically, I realized that in order to have the experience, I had to eliminate what I had done.

I think that, to some degree, this is part of my character as a designer: To keep moving and not get stuck in my own past. This is what I try very hard to do.

I think at that moment in my life, I found a peculiar path: To continually discard a lot of the things that I knew how to do in favor of finding out what I didn't. I think this is the way you stay alive professionally.

I don't think I liked this idea of destroying your universe at the end of every day in order to start again. But it seems to me that it is a very profound principle.

I think a lot of people collect memory and accomplishments and use these things to remind them of what they have done in their lives.

I do that. I look back occasionally, though not that often. But I have had a very peculiar career in the profession.

You said memory was treacherous. Why?

Think about someone who has gone back to where

he once lived and discovered that it was a third of the size he thought it was. Memory is treacherous; you can't depend on it. It is basically always recreated to reinforce your anxiety or to make yourself look better, but whatever actually did happen is totally susceptible to subjective interpretation. I absolutely don't trust my memory.

How important was financial success when you first started out?

Not at all. I never had the model of financial success as being the reason to work. When I was at Push Pin, none of the partners made enough money to live on. It took ten years for us to make as much as a junior art director in an agency. We were making $65 a week! But money has never been a motivating force in my work. I am very happy to have made enough money to live as well as I do, but I never thought of money as a reason to work. For me, work was about survival. I had to work in order to have any sense of being human. If I wasn't working or making something, I was very nervous and unstable.

Why is that?

Because for whatever reason, work is what I do. I recently read a study of happiness. Those people who are most happy are those who are most fully engaged in their work, whatever that work happens to be. So it isn't a surprise to me that so much of my satisfaction and happiness in life comes out of my relationship to my work. And I still have the feeling that I have enormous opportunities and possibilities. There is always so much more to understand about the nature of communicating and design and color. You reach a point in your life when you realize that you know nothing about color or shape!

Or you don't know anything about anything!

And that is a great feeling: when you feel the possibility of learning. It's a terrible feeling to feel

you can't learn or have reached the end of
your potential.

*I think it's interesting that you weren't concerned
about survival or making a living—that doing the
work was more important than security.*

Well, somebody said—and it's one of the principles
of the New Age, but I also think it's true—that if
you perceive the universe as being a universe of
abundance, then it will be. If you think of the universe as one of scarcity, then it will be. And I never
thought of the universe as one of scarcity. I always
thought that there was enough of everything to go
around—that there are enough ideas in the universe
and enough nourishment.

A lot of people I know think the universe is
one of scarcity, and if they don't get enough money
or enough fame, it's because there isn't enough to
go around. I think there is more than enough of
everything to go around. If the world could shift
this consciousness, the sense of abundance would
be overwhelming.

It's like the old story of primitive societies:
When these groups are living at the edge of survival, everyone eats, and there is enough food for
everyone. As soon as there is a surplus—this is
absolutely characteristic of primitive tribes and
everything else—people start starving. Because
as soon as there is surplus, people begin to horde.
It is a simple proposition, but almost universally
true from an anthropological point of view—with
surplus, comes starvation.

*Over the years, I've talked with people about your
ethical critique, "12 Steps on the Graphic Designer's
Road to Hell." One of the comments that I hear from
young designers is that when you can't pay your rent,
it's a lot easier to go to Step 3* ["Designing a crest for
a new vineyard to suggest that it has been in business for a long time"] *or Step 4* ["Designing a jacket

for a book whose sexual content you find personally repellent"]. *But if you're in a position where you're well-known and financially secure, then you don't have to worry about survival.*

As a designer, you've reached a point in your life where you have an innate sense of "No matter what happens, I will survive." Some people have that innate sense of survival without being at a point where they are well-known and financially secure, and other people I know are well-known and financially secure, but don't have even a smidgen of innate security.

It is a fascinating conundrum. Another way it's put very often is this: Do you perceive you live your life through love or fear? They are very different manifestations. My favorite quote is by the English novelist Iris Murdoch. She said, "Love is the very difficult understanding that something other than yourself is real." I like the idea that all that love is, is acknowledging another's reality.

Acknowledging that the world exists, and that you are not the only participant in it, is a profound step. The impulse towards narcissism or self-interest is so profound, particularly when you have a worry of injury or fear. It's very hard to move beyond the idea that there is not enough to go around, to move beyond that sense of "I better get mine before anybody else takes it away from me."

You started your career with a strong sense of "work first, and survival will come." What advice would you give to students who are just graduating?

I often say that the most important thing in those first ten years out of school is not to take a job that will determine your entire life—which happens to a lot of people. They start working for a magazine and they start by assisting, and then they become a junior art director, and then an art director, and ten years later, they're married and have children. And then the option to change course has been reduced to almost nothing. So you have to be careful. One of the great things at Push Pin was that we did not earn a lot of money, and it did not improve our living conditions. Once your living condition is improved, it's very hard to move back from it.

When you're working on a project, how do you know when you've created something that's good or successful?

Well, remember that I have been doing this for well over a half a century. This is not an amateur effort on my part!

For one thing—and here you can use memory—you can look at the work you've done in the past and gauge its effectiveness, its power, and its grace. But you have to be tough-minded. You must be able to self-evaluate. You have to be very tough about your work in order to get anywhere. Like everything else, the issue surrounds narcissism and self-protection. You just have to be able to look and be able to assess what is not very good or not as good as you hoped. What I also find interesting is that as you progress in this field—as opposed to most other fields—there are some things you can't do anymore. I can't do the things I was able to do 30 years ago.

For example?

Certain kinds of drawing and certain ways of putting things together that are more physically demanding. And my mind has changed, too. My ideas have changed. As Charles Olson said in the poem, "Maximus, to himself," "I have had to learn the simplest things last." Over the last couple of years, I have been learning about those simple things. The work has circled from a modernist education in high school and at Cooper Union, then a repudiation of modernism and simplicity, and now a return to the idea that you can be powerful, direct, and simple. I don't have an ideological stance about complexity and simplicity.

When a chef is tested, they ask him to cook an omelet. It's a very simple test, not how to make a complex stew using truffles. A perfect omelet involves knowing how much air to get into the eggs, how much heat to apply to the pan, and how to turn it over cleanly. It turns out to be a very profound test. You realize that the standard can be reduced to very simple acts. But these have to be perfectly produced. At this point in my life, I am most interested in not repeating what I already know. I still hope to find things that I don't know and can struggle with.

I had a good friend who was a very good designer and was very indebted to the ideas of money, success, and the rewards of accomplishment. And then, like everybody, he began to fade, and he was so bitter about the fact that the world was no longer coming to him for what he had done all his life. And he became uninterested in working any more. He lost all his appetite for doing things. And I realized that the focus of his life was about the consequences of his work rather than the work itself. And I think that is a kind of sadness. Because it leaves you with nothing. Because eventually— particularly in an industry that deals so much with fashion—you are going to be out of favor some day.

So what do you attribute your longevity to?

I don't know. Just staying at the desk turning out the work and trying to do it as well as I can. I am also a very persistent man: a stubborn, persistent man. And the reward is still the same reward: doing things that have quality, that are still powerful, and that reach people. And, of course, the sheer joy of doing it. I love coming in to my office and working.

Tell me about the peaks and valleys in your career.

I think that the worst period of my life was the first year of doing *New York*. I did not know how to do it! I was producing horrible, horrible magazines week after week. The editorial team didn't know what

HOW TO THINK LIKE A GREAT GRAPHIC DESIGNER

they were doing, either. We knew how we were going to do the first issue, and after that, we were surprised that there was going to be a second one, which was due at the printers a few days later. Doing a weekly is tough. And prior to that experience, I had never really been an art director at a magazine. I had done a lot of magazine work, but never art-directed.

We got off to a shaky start. And I did a lot of bad, bad work, and it was public. Every week, people would say, "Oh boy, have you ever seen such an ugly—..." For a year, it was very embarrassing. It was very hard to fix while we were moving so fast. Eventually, I began figuring it all out, and the magazine found its voice.

Are you ever insecure about anything now?

Insecure? What is there to feel secure about? There is no security in the world, or in life. I don't mind living with some ambiguity and realizing that eventually, everything changes. I tend to be somebody who wants recurrence in life. It seems that everything I have ever done, I have been doing for 50 years. I have been working in this building where my office is since 1965. I have been married for 50 years. I have been teaching for about 48 years.

So I guess there is a certain security that I have always sought by making things recur. You have certain things in your life that you do all your life. I don't think I've been very adventurous in my life.

Is there anything you would have liked to have done or still hope to do?

Nothing.

How would you define "adventurous"?

Being physically adventurous—doing things like snorkeling and water-skiing and putting myself at risk.

My adventure has all been in my mind. The great adventure has been thinking. I love to think about things. I think that the lack of drama in my life has produced a platform for me to be fundamentally adventurous in my thinking.

I have very few "interests." I have not been to the movies in 12 years. I listen to music at home, but I don't go to concerts. I just read and work. That's all I do. And I teach.

And I find it all thrilling. I love to teach, I love the experience of teaching. I love the response people have to teaching. And I love feeling useful in teaching. And I think I have become a good teacher by understanding that what you teach is what you are. You don't teach by telling people things.

Can you elaborate on that?

[Giorgio] Morandi was one of my first great teachers. We never talked about art during the years I was there in Italy. He never suggested what I should do with my art. Nothing. But I saw his devotion to his work and how he was willing to teach a high school–level class in rudimentary etching, and then, after class, he would promptly leave and spend the rest of the day painting. He was totally devoted to his work.

He used to tell me, "If you want to paint like—insert favorite painter—you must put in your time." His idea of standing for something, of having a stance in life that is immediately conveyed to others, was totally understood. The minute he would walk in a room, we got it. There is an element of that which is didactic, but he was always conveying ideas even when he wasn't "teaching" per se.

I believe that you convey your ideas by the authenticity of your being. Not by glibly telling someone what to do or how to do it. I believe that this is why so much teaching is ineffective. People are not what they teach, and the students immediately know it. Good teaching is merely having an encounter with someone who has an idea of what life is that you admire and want to emulate.

What do you think you stand for?

I think I stand for an attempt to think responsibly about the practice of design in terms of its effects on society. I don't say that self-righteously. I believe that you have to think about the consequences of what you do. I try to be conscious about this, and raise the issue wherever and whenever I can. I also think I stand for an openness about what the design profession can be, and how things beyond the practice affect and modify both society and the way we think about design.

You started the "Designism" movement, which stresses designers' work for social change. Do you feel that we are not doing enough?

I wouldn't characterize designers as being different from everybody else in the universe. I think, to some degree, everybody suffers from similar issues. I think everybody should be more generous and more concerned about the effect they have on the world. Being a designer is also about being a good citizen. What does it mean to be a good citizen? It means caring about what's going on and taking a role. Designers have the unique opportunity to have a different role than an average person who doesn't have access to production and manufacturing in the same physical way as a designer does. So there is more opportunity and more responsibility.

The reality of being in the world and caring about that world is ultimately in our own self-interest. When you create a competitive and acrimonious environment, you suffer. If you play that game, then you have to pay the consequences on a personal level.

Do you think the part of the brain that seeks commu-
nity is awakened by communal brand experiences like
MySpace, YouTube, or the iPod?

Yes. But there is a dark side to this. People develop communities that define themselves and isolate them from others. This leads to a kind of estrangement from everyone else. And before you know it, there's a class or status war, or some other sense that we're more important because of our desires, or a sense of betterment because we have good taste, or because we earn more money. That collective identification quickly turns into a way of excluding others from humanity. We have to be so cautious of this. It is an endless cycle of human history. A collective consciousness develops within a tribe, and everyone outside becomes worthless—it's a prevailing pattern in humanity.

Did you ever have a vision that this would be the life
you would be leading?

This is the only life I could have imagined for myself. Since that day with the paper bag, I have not deviated. I wanted to spend every day of my life making something, and that is all I have ever done. It has been a totally unwavering path.

Paula Scher

Manhattan's visual canvas is defined by an electric, exhilarating collage, whether in the sensory overload of 42nd Street's LED screens, the handmade signs painted for local businesses, or the advertisements towering over the cityscape.

Paula Scher's compositions have made an unmistakable imprint on the visual symphony of New York and American popular culture. Her work for arts organizations such as The Public Theater showcase her ability to capture the vitality of her subject matter with heady assemblages of type and image. Her record covers for Atlantic and CBS Records from the '70s remain classics of the genre, their intelligence and wit poignant to this day.

Paula joined Pentagram as partner in 1991, and she has since completed projects including a redesign of the Citibank identity, show openers for PBS, book design for Jon Stewart's America, and environmental signage for a host of clients. She is perhaps best known for her use of type, but she tells me that it wasn't until after college that she came to understand typography. "I didn't seek it," she explains. "It found me."

Paula defines design as "the art of planning." This description seems particularly apt, as her design and typographic explorations have increasingly moved from the two-dimensional page to the three-dimensional scale of architecture and buildings. If only we could enjoy the visceral delights of living in a city planned and composed entirely by Paula Scher.

What was your first creative memory?

I made a mural in sixth grade. It was a transportation mural. I remember it because it earned me some praise, though I'm sure I did a lot of things before sixth grade. But at that time, I got to paint a transportation mural showing a highway with cars on it. I made the highway with the traffic lanes "backwards," and my teacher said, "Oh, it can be an English highway."

When you were younger, what did you want to be when you grew up?

A singer, dancer, piano player, and bareback rider— I wanted to perform.

I have a theory that graphic designers secretly wish they were rock stars. When did you know you wanted to be a graphic designer?

When I went to college, I didn't know what graphic design was. It wasn't until my junior year that I discovered it. And I think I wanted to study design because the school I went to taught a very Basel-oriented basic graphic design course, which was "white on white": taking pieces of white paper and laying them over each other. But I was very sloppy; I was horrible at it. I was terrible at anything that involved rubber cement and rubber cement pick-up. These were things I just couldn't accomplish. I went to the design department to be an illustrator, not a designer, because I didn't think I had the skills to be a designer, whereas illustration seemed to be more expressive.

Did you have aspirations to be an illustrator or designer specifically, or was that something that happened more serendipitously? Was it something you knew you were going to do?

I always knew I was going to make things. I was compelled to make things. I wanted to make wonderful things, things that other people liked, things that were important and mattered. I wanted to do this because I liked the act of doing it, and I wanted that form of approval, and so I would have a way of expressing myself.

At first, when I was at college, I really didn't understand typography at all. I actually learned it on the job; I didn't learn it in college. I didn't seek it. It found me. At one point I had a teacher who gave me some very, very critical advice. He told me to find one thing you can do. And only do that. Be the best at it, no matter how narrow it is. And get rid of all the stuff you don't do well. And I found that to be an amazing piece of advice. I go back to it all the time.

How would you define the term "graphic design"?

I would start first with the term "design." If you look it up in the dictionary, it says, "a plan." And I see design as the art of planning. There's an implication in graphic design that it involves both planning and something graphic, something produced, something that may have breadth or have words or images attached, or have some impact. It's a nebulous description of design. I actually prefer to say I'm a visual planner.

Do you find that people understand what you mean when you say that?

No. They don't understand until they see it. I believe that people are far more aware of the impact or import of design than they realize, though they don't know how to describe it. I recently joined the Art Commission of the City of New York. They created a seat for a graphic designer, which they never had included before. They did it because they were confronted with so many sign systems that they had to deal with—and environmental projects that had gone awry—that they realized they needed a graphic designer's expertise.

When something like this happens, you know that design has reached a broader audience and understanding. Serving with the Commission has been terrific. There's an artist, architect, engineer, and an art historian, and there are two seats from the Metropolitan Museum and the Brooklyn Museum. It's our responsibility to sign off on every building to be built in New York City that receives public funding. It has to go through the Art Commission. It's totally fascinating.

Do you consider yourself to be successful?

It depends on how you define success.

How do you define success?

I think I'm successful in certain ways. I think that I'm lucky in that I like what I do, and I get to do it. That is a factor in how I see myself as successful.

I consider the fact that I have been able to continue to grow a very important part of how I perceive success. To me, success is not about money, it's about what I design. If I get up every day with the optimism that I have the capacity for growth, then that's success for me.

Do you consider yourself a confident person?

When I was young, I was not a confident person, but I presented myself as if I was. I was cocky, and I had a certain kind of attitude and panache that I rolled out when I needed it. But it was a piece of armor and a house of cards. After 25 years of working, I think I've gotten much more confident. I am more comfortable in my own skin. I don't look around so much for approval. I find myself comfortable enough to be myself.

How would you describe yourself?

Short. Little. Perfectly formed. Little person with a big mouth.

How would your husband describe you?

Probably exactly the same.

How would Michael Bierut describe you?

The same.

Do you have a process that you use when you're designing? A way that you initiate a project, a way that you work through a problem?

It's a little difficult to say what I do first. I don't do anything in any particular order. There's a certain amount of intuitive thinking that goes into everything. It's so hard to describe how things happen intuitively. I can describe it as a computer and a slot machine. I have a pile of stuff in my brain, a pile of stuff from all the books I've read and all the movies I've seen. Every piece of artwork I've ever looked at. Every conversation that's inspired me, every piece of street art I've seen along the way. Anything I've purchased, rejected, loved, hated. It's all in there. It's all on one side of the brain.

And on the other side of the brain is a specific brief that comes from my understanding of the project and says, okay, this solution is made up of A, B, C, and D. And if you pull the handle on the slot machine, they sort of run around in a circle, and what you hope is that those three cherries line up, and the cash comes out.

When you're thinking this way, is it something you're doing alone, or with a lot of other people?

I could be doing it right now. I'm doing it right here. My day is very packed, and it's filled with many interruptions. I'm thinking about the brief while I'm in an open space with tons of people, in the office, with telephones, my staff, while gossiping with my partners, while thinking about what's going on in the world, during whatever's going on at that moment—plus the brief.

I am conscious of resolving the brief, but I don't think about it too hard. I allow the subconscious part of my brain to work. That's the accumulation of my whole life. That is what's going on in the other side of my brain, trying to align with this very logical brief.

And I'm allowing that to flow freely, so that the cherries can line up in the slot machine. I don't know when that's going to happen. I've had periods of time when the cherries never line up, and that's scary, because then you have to rely on tricks you already have up your sleeve—the tricks in your knowledge from other jobs. And very often you rely on this.

But mostly what you want to do is invent. And to invent, you have to take the odd and the strange combination of the years of knowledge and experience on one side of the brain, and on the other side, the necessity for the brief to make sense. And you're drawing from that knowledge to make an analogy and to find a way to solve a problem, to find a means of moving forward—in a new way—things you've already done.

When you succeed, it's fantastic. It doesn't always happen. But every so often, you take a bunch of stuff from one side of your head, and a very logical list of stuff from the other side, and through that osmosis you're finding a new way to look at a problem and resolve a situation.

How are you able to evaluate your own success at solving a problem?

It's very hard. I know when I make a breakthrough. There's a moment of "Eureka!" And that comes from knowing what previously existed in that area or arena and pushing it forward. If it's a magazine, there's a history of magazines; if it's an identity, there's a history of identities. If it's an identity for a certain type of business, there's a history of identities for that certain type of business.

Generally, there's a paradigm of what things look like in any arena. What you want to be able to do is find a new way to stretch that paradigm forward, to break its own mold. Sometimes to do that, you borrow from another area. That's why I like to work on all different types of projects.

Right now, I'm designing a building as a user's manual. I'm taking a form of print and marrying it to a three-dimensional system. Then the knowledge "over there" informs something new "over here." That is when it's possible to make a breakthrough. And that is really what I want out of design. I want to create unexpected things set in a way that makes logical sense. I want to reinterpret how things can be put together. This changes the expectations of what is possible.

What do you do when you experience the feeling of "eureka" about a design solution and your client doesn't? How are you able to convince them to see things your way?

I do that in a variety of ways, and I'm not always successful. The best way to be successful with this is to be doing the job for free. Very often, I do a lot of work for nonprofit organizations. I literally donate the work—so that I can make a breakthrough. If I'm doing a job for free, they're not challenging me, they're accepting what I create. If they pay me, they have a right to participate.

Occasionally, we make a breakthrough with a very well-paying client. With one particular client, I made a presentation before I showed any work and logically explained why they had to do what I was presenting. I proved my thesis before presenting creative solutions. I've done that a number of times, and I'm getting better at it. It's a lot of work, but I've been trying to do this more and more. I know I have a tendency to jump to an answer without taking the time to express the logical steps.

Back when I was in high school, I took geometry. In the class, we were taught to write a theorem to show how we got to an answer. But I just rushed and wrote the answer. I don't know why or how I knew the answer, I just did. I couldn't explain it, and my teacher insisted that I prove it out. This type of proof is a struggle for me. But slowly I've been getting better at explaining to people why "this" is the answer.

I recently did a job, and my clients wanted me to tweak something. I thought it was an awful idea, and I didn't want to do it. They came back and asked me to tell them why I thought it was so awful, and why they shouldn't make the change. I made a very serious presentation articulating why I thought what they wanted to do was so bad, and why it was so off-target. It was very persuasive. After the presentation, they realized how poor the idea was. So I'm getting better at this. But that doesn't make it easy.

Would you say your work is more intuitive or intellectual?

I think it's both. Actually, this is what I think my husband would say about me: that I'm emotional and analytical at the same time.

So how do you know when a project is done? How do you know when you're finished?

That is hard. Sometimes I'm done because I run out of time. That's as good a way as any. I've done very good things that way. Sometimes a deadline gets you to stop. I love deadlines. Sometimes a project is done because you've done too much and you've made it worse. And you have to stop and go back.

Sometimes you're never done. But I think that it's dangerous to have any kind of satisfaction. You always have to be striving to improve on the next project. The next project has to be what you're aspiring for, not what you've just completed—you've already done that.

When you look at the work you've created, in the last five or ten years, do you feel that it's good enough, or do you feel that it's too soon to tell?

It's not a question of just looking at the work; it's a question of understanding where I was when I did the work, the context of when I did it, and where I am now. I find that you have to continually renew, that growth is what matters. You can't do the same thing for five years. You have to get rid of it. It doesn't matter anymore. Just let it go, even if it's your signature. Even if everybody expects you to do it. Try to find another way to walk. It's easy to say in theory, but harder to do in practice.

For me, that's why the breadth, the core, matters. Because when I change what I'm doing from editorial packaging to environmental design to identity to motion graphics to some form of Web work—as long as I can do that—it's going to take my work in another direction. Particularly because I've been practicing for 25 years, I have to keep walking forward. I can't look at the past and worry about whether it's good or bad. It's critical for me to move on to the next project, to discover the next thing.

How do you find those new things?

You need to be logical. You have to go out and get the kind of projects that allow this to happen for you. I pay overhead. I maintain a staff. I'm not working in some ivory tower where I get to create work for myself. I'm working in the real word. The projects dictate when I can go to the extreme, and, to a degree, when I can invent.

Are you able to hold on to success and happiness,
or are they fleeting experience?

I don't even know that I feel it. Half the time I can't even believe it.

Do you worry a lot?

I worry about my future.

In what way?

I'm 58 years old; I don't know how long I can keep it going.

What do you do when you need a role model?
Where do you look for inspiration? I'm not talking
about movies or books, I'm talking about people.

People inspiration is hard. There are a few women who have achieved an enormous amount. There aren't a lot of them. You know, Stefan Sagmeister told me that no one has a breakthrough in their fifties. But I did. So now he says no one's had a breakthrough in their sixties.

So he's setting your bar. Are you afraid of anything?

Being over the hill.

Do you really think that will happen? I mean, honestly?

It's inevitable; it will happen sooner or later. You can't defy that forever.

What do you think is the secret to your staying power?

I don't think I have a very big opinion of myself.

You're just driven? Trying to prove yourself?

If you think you're only as good as your last job—which I do—there's more to be done. I know what I did today. I know exactly what level it's at, and there are all kinds of problems and compromises that I must negotiate. Things that have to be held on to, things that have to be protected to make something move forward. And it's very, very, very hard work. It doesn't have anything to do with fame. It has to do with doing it every day.

That is all that matters—nothing else matters. I believe that we all want to leave something behind that is really, truly terrific. And we have this finite amount of time to accomplish it. Everything else is unimportant. I like that you're doing this book because what motivates it is a really important discussion about accomplishments in graphic design. The accoutrements, and the awards, and my picture in a book don't matter. What matters is the next project. If you're sitting back and saying, "Gee, that was wonderful," that is death. You're killing yourself. You can't do that. You can't do that to yourself.

If you could fantasize for a minute, it's five years from now. We're that much closer to our imminent demise. How do you see yourself, your life? Are you painting, are you still designing? Are you still at Pentagram? What are you doing?

I am not really sure. I'm facing that right now, and I am really, totally confused. What I think is terrific is that I actually have the possibility to paint full-time. I would do it. On the other hand, when faced with the choice, I wouldn't want to give up designing because I really love design. I really love designing. I guess I'm a very lucky woman.

Stefan Sagmeister

Stefan Sagmeister and I nearly got arrested together. While working on a conceptual design project utilizing my office in the Empire State Building, Stefan dangled out of my 17th-floor window with a sign that simply read, "OVER." It never occurred to me that the crowd below would think that the sign read, "IT'S OVER" and was the parting message of a jumper. When hordes of police and press showed up, accompanied by every fire truck and ambulance in the vicinity, it dawned on me that the whole of Manhattan was watching the flawless execution of a true master at work.

That's the thing about Stefan Sagmeister. He has the unique ability to turn life into art. He makes you look, and then, when you take it all in, he makes you wonder why it took you so long to notice what he's known all along—that "you can have an art experience in front of a Rembrandt . . . or in front of a piece of graphic design."

Stefan is the closest thing the design field has to both a conceptual fine artist and a rock star. Yet even with all of the accolades and fanfare, Stefan is humble, down-to-earth, and incredibly generous with his time. He and I conducted this dialogue both by e-mail and in person. The result makes for an interview that is equal parts insight, inspiration, and performance art.

What was your first creative memory?

When I was eight, I remember having to paint various blue and yellow watercolors on boards, then subsequently cutting the boards up into tiny little squares, and pasting these to form an illustration of an exploding yellow balloon in a blue bathtub. The entire concoction was assigned by our minimalist art teacher, Herr Pfitzer. Mine was deemed not very good.

When you were little, what did you want to be when you grew up?

A Catholic priest.

I hear you're thinking about taking another year off without clients. What made you decide to do this in the first place?

I would say there were numerous reasons. Being bored was probably the simplest one; I was simply bored. We'd been in the music business for seven years, and I was bored with the process of designing CD covers and visualizing music. Actually, I was more frustrated with the fact that we had three clients on every job: the record label, the management, and the band. And we were often the little ball that was thrown between those three big entities. Also, Ed Fella had recently visited the studio, and I was very impressed with his experimental typography sketchbooks, what he refers to as "Exit Art." I also think Tibor Kalman's death had something to do with it.

In what way?

It was a reminder of what a short time we have here, and how important it is to do the work that you feel you should do. In previous years, I had worked in Hong Kong and Vienna and New York and in between those various cities; I always had a little time before starting a new job. This allowed me to constantly rethink and challenge what I was doing.

After seven years at the studio, I knew I still loved New York very much and that I had no real reason to move anywhere else. But I wanted to create a little artificial gap to allow for reconsidering what I was doing. I also realized I was having less and less fun in the office, and knew I had to do something about that; I knew if my happiness in the studio went away, everything would go down the drain. It has been almost six years since I've been back to work. I now have a fairly good perspective about whether or not this was worthwhile. And I would say very enthusiastically, yes, it was worthwhile.

Were there any moments during this year off when you were worried about not being able to make a living when you came back?

During the year after I made the decision, I didn't worry very much, because I had already made the decision. But before, very much so. I thought that I would be forgotten in a second. I worried that all of my clients might leave and not come back, and I would have to start up all over again. But I also thought it might be an interesting thing for me to start up all over again.

What was the most important thing you learned in that year?

I think there were numerous things I learned. I realized that the anger I sometimes had toward clients was not necessarily about the clients. It was within me. When I didn't have clients to tend to, I was just as angry, or not angry, as I was before. One of the things I realized that year was that there was a certain amount of anger in me that was fairly un-client-related.

What makes you angry?

Disorganization. People who are not interested in what they're doing. But I don't think that I'm angrier than any other person. I think there is a certain amount of anger in every human being. And also happiness. I spoke to Danny Gilbert about this. He is a psychologist from Harvard who has done a lot of research on happiness. All his studies show that outside events have surprisingly little to do with our happiness. He said that with a few exceptions—like the death of a child—there is almost nothing that happens in our lives that has a profound impact on our lives six months after the event. I also think I answered an important question for myself that year.

What do you mean?

In the very beginning of the year, I thought that I might rather be a movie director than a graphic designer. For me, this seemed like an intriguing option to pursue. Having been somewhat close to the movie industry—directing a music video for Lou Reed and having a number of friends who are in the business—I was not very naïve about doing something like this. I figured it would likely be a ten-year process until I could hope to have made something I would be happy with. I started to map out how those ten years would look: What I would do; how I would learn; which school I could go to; and how I could make it happen financially.

As intriguing as I found the process, I could not help but wonder what would happen if I went through this process—this learning of a new language—and after ten years, I had nothing to say in it? Then it occurred to me that it might be smarter if I stuck with the language I already knew and tried to really say something with it. I remember writing this down in my diary, and I challenged myself to try this. And the whole series "Things I've Learned in My Life So Far" came out of this process.

It seems to me that you're the kind of person who could succeed at anything, if you put your mind to it. Do you really doubt that you could have been

successful as a filmmaker if you chose to pursue it
with all of your heart?

I'll never know until I put ten years into it. But I think I've found what I want to do in design. Just yesterday, I read an article in a very old issue of *The New Yorker* about an Indian man. He was speaking about karma and what it is like to find out what you are really put on this earth to do. For me, the mix of what we deal with as designers—the mix of words, images, and messages—this is what I was meant to do.

I like the fact that design is audience-related. I like the fact that it's not "art" and that you're typically collaborating with other people.

There is a host of particularities within design that I enjoy. I like to work with clients. But only designing is difficult for me. I can't sit down every day and actually design for ten hours. I can design for two or three hours. Then I am very happy to do other things.

In the design world, you are a big rock star. How does
that make you feel?

I would say two things: "Rock star" has become quite a generic expression for many things people do. A friend of mine recently referred to another friend of mine as a "rock star" because she had an easy time delivering a baby. Secondly, design is our little world. Which is—and I'm very aware of this— a wonderful kind of "fame" to have. As a designer, you're very much in charge of your fame. You go to a conference, everybody knows you, likes you, your ego is filled up. You get out of the conference, and you can do whatever you want and nobody bothers you.

Having been around many actual rock stars, I've seen the different characters, and there are some rock stars out there who truly enjoy it. Steven Tyler of Aerosmith loves being a rock star. Others really suffer through it. They have become famous through a true love of music, and they basically want to be left alone. I see sides of that in Lou Reed. Fame can become a real pain in the ass. As a designer, you have none of that. You feel like you have only the positive aspects of it, and none of the negative. And as I have said before: "A famous designer is like a famous electrician."

When did you realize that you wanted to be a graphic designer?

At 16, when I started to write for a small maga-zine and discovered that I liked gluing the layouts together and handwriting the headlines—the *e*'s were always missing on our donated Letraset sheets. I was also a member of a terrible band and stared at record covers for hours on end— as an excuse to avoid rehearsing.

When did you realize you had design talent?

I feel that talent is the implemented desire to excel at something. I had a desire to be good at design when I was 18 or 19 and first entered art school in Vienna.

Did you have an experience since then when you knew you had reached a level of being a really good designer? Did you ever have a moment when you thought, "Aha! This is what I wanted. This is what I was hoping for"?

Rarely. Perhaps here and there. Occasionally, when I have completed something and it comes back from the printer. I think there's one reason why being a designer fits me well. I'm very much changing with the opinion of the audience. Very much like a wet-finger politician. I put my finger up in the air to see which way the wind blows. I think this would be very detrimental to my work if I were a fine artist. But in the field of graphic design—where you are

always designing something for an audience—
it works very well to be this way.

*Why do you think it would be detrimental if you were
a fine artist?*

I think the expectation is that fine artists basically
work for themselves, and the audience gets whatever they can from it. I'm sure there are fine artists
out there who keep the audience in mind when
they work. But it's not the accepted trajectory of the
profession. Conversely, it's very clear in design that
what we do needs to be seen and understood by
an audience.

How would you define the term "graphic design"?

Surely you must be joking. Smarter people have shot
their little toe off over this.

Come on, give it a try.

If you insist, how about:
Graphic design is the work that is made by
a graphic designer.

Or:

The combination of visual and written
expression of an idea, process, and system
for the betterment of client interests, human
locomotion, not excluding the recent trend of
a lower x-height among Dutch typographers.

*Do you ever feel insecure about things? Do you ever
worry about not being good enough?*

I think I worry more about certain pieces not being
good enough or my work being mediocre. Sometimes I get stuck, and I can't seem to push the
work further.

What do you do when that happens?

It depends on what kind of shape I'm in. If I'm in a

very energetic shape, I might have the guts to throw it out and start anew. If I'm not, I might let it go and produce something mediocre or slightly above mediocre. It depends on how strong I am at that given time. I assume this happens to many people. It is always easiest to do things that you've done before. Though sometimes it can be good to repeat yourself.

Why do you feel that way? In what way is it good to repeat yourself?

Sometimes it's good to repeat something, and to push it. When I first started out, my mantra in the studio was that for every project, we had to try out something totally new. Which of course proved humanly impossible fairly quickly. It was not supportable. And I don't think it is supportable by anybody. So the studio has settled into multiple ways of working.

Sometimes we do something totally new, but sometimes it's okay to use handwriting again.

There is a proper way to develop things, but sometimes it's difficult to decide: Are you just repeating yourself, or are you doing something really different?

You said sometimes you just let something go that might be mediocre. How often do you think that you do that?

Probably quite often. If I looked over the work we completed last year, I would say I am really happy with about three projects. And we worked on at least 15 projects. So that means I let something go 12 times. But I don't separate the good things from the bad, and I know that many studios do. One company I know says, "This one's for the meal, this one's for the reel." Because I keep my studio so small, there's not very much we have to do for the meal.

Now, to be clear, those 12 projects that I'm referring to, I'm not embarrassed by them. Most of them have good content, and I would say that all of them were done for clients who have a product that is worthwhile, and they all had a right to be interesting. But for one reason or another, they are not quite where the other three are.

Do you find that you have a process for initiating your design work?

Yes. There are several processes, to be combined differently for every project.

They include list-making; switching from one project to another; going alone into a café with nothing to read and nobody to meet, thus winding up like a lonely fool and being shamed into working (stole this technique from director Steven Soderbergh); and starting a project where the seed of the idea has absolutely nothing to do with the project, like designing a campaign to promote literacy using the word "air-conditioner"—a technique developed by Edward de Bono.

Do you turn down a lot of work?

Yes. That's a function of a small studio. Roughly, we can do a dozen jobs a year. Roughly. We are now at job number 140, and we have been in business for 12 or 13 years. Of course, the nice thing about this is we can pick the ones that seem the best.

Do you regret anything?

Not accepting the Zadie Smith *On Beauty* cover design when it later turned out to be my favorite novel of that year.

Do you ever see yourself wanting to have a bigger studio or joining forces with anyone else?

No. Before I opened the studio, I worked for many companies, large and small. I feel like I've gotten my dose of the large corporate world, of the midsized corporate world, and of the smallish corporate world. And I have worked in studios that were ten,

20, 30 people. And I feel that when I look at the work emerging from any of these entities, the really good work was most often done by three people. When 20 people were involved, it mostly sucked. So for me, it never seems that size works in favor of the client.

From my own perspective, a small studio has numerous advantages. You have low overhead, so you can be financially independent. You are also able to remain a designer, something that many of my friends have lost as their businesses grew to 10 or 20 people. I like doing the little bit of management that my small company needs, but I don't want to do it full-time. I don't want to become a full-time design manager.

Is there anything that you haven't done yet that you want to do?

In design?

In life.

Oh yes, there are a couple of things on my list that I haven't done. I haven't driven a truck through Antarctica. I haven't moved to Sri Lanka for a year. I would like to do both. In design, two things I have not done include designing a CD cover for King Crimson, even though we don't do music packaging anymore. King Crimson is a band that was close to my heart for a very, very long time. And I would love to work on a big, worldwide brand, but only if I would have access to the decision-maker.

The only disadvantage of the small studio is that most very, very large branding projects tend to go to very large international firms. From my point of view, this is entirely misbegotten. If you look at the successful brands worldwide, almost all of the successful identities have been designed by single entities, from Nike to Apple to IBM. It's partly because they come from a time when Paul Rand or Saul Bass designed them.

I'm very, very well aware that branding is much more than logo design. At the same time, what international consultancies do now is primarily centered on consulting and not design, though they pretend otherwise. These consultancies would much rather be out of the design business. However, when you sit down with the owners or with the founders of these consultancies at a bar after a conference, it's apparent what they do. And everything else that they claim they are doing is certainly not at the core of what they are doing. If you look at a brand holistically, the consultancies do not do what is probably the most important thing that a brand really does.

What do you think that is?

They have no influence or impact on the quality of the product. The quality of the product has much more influence than what the designer does. Every conference I go to, people talk about the same products: It's always the iPod; it's always Starbucks; it's always the successful products from the last decade. Despite the fact that these are design conferences, there are constantly all these theories being presented about how the companies that make these products have figured out branding. But what it really comes down to is the fact that these companies have figured out how to make a really good product.

If you look at the advertising and branding budgets of these companies, they are tiny. If you look at the advertising and branding budget of Starbucks compared to McDonald's, it's a small, tiny percentage. I think the consumer is pretty smart in making choices based on quality. However, what designers do has an unbelievable impact on a couple of sectors where the consumer doesn't know the difference.

For example?

Water. Vodka. There is no way for the consumer

to tell one water from another, or one vodka from another. Whatever we do—be it the advertising, be it the bottle, or be it the logo on the bottle—it really makes a difference, because it is the only thing for the consumer to evaluate while making the decision about what to buy. When the consumer really does know the difference—with cars, or with a cup of coffee, for example—what we do becomes fairly insignificant.

So if you could work for any brand at all, what brand would you want to work for?

It probably would be one that has worldwide distribution. It would be a good product—perhaps one that I use myself, and I'm in favor of; and a product that doesn't do any harm. Verizon would be a good candidate.

When was the last time you cried?

A video of a live performance of Iggy Pop, shown in front of the Peter Saville exhibit at Laforet Museum in Tokyo: The concert must have been from the early '80s, after the release of *Lust for Life*. In the video, the band starts by playing "The Passenger."

The guitar goes:
dadadam, dadadam, dadadam, dadadam,
dadadam, dadadam, dadadam, dadadam,
The audience goes nuts, it's Iggy's big hit.

The guitar goes:
dadadam, dadadam, dadadam, dadadam,
dadadam, dadadam, dadadam, dadadam,
Iggy is supposed to join in, but just stands toward the back of the stage instead, smiling.

The guitar goes:
dadadam, dadadam, dadadam, dadadam,
dadadam, dadadam, dadadam, dadadam,
Iggy smiles, the audience goes nuts.

The guitar goes:

dadadam, dadadam, dadadam, dadadam,
dadadam, dadadam, dadadam, dadadam,

Iggy waits, the audience wants him to join in, you
see them get up on their toes, they need him to join,
Iggy waits.

The guitar goes:

dadadam, dadadam, dadadam, dadadam,
dadadam, dadadam, dadadam, dadadam,

Iggy slowly walks to the front of the stage, surely
now it can only be seconds away, surely the audience
will get some relief.

The guitar goes:

dadadam, dadadam, dadadam, dadadam,
dadadam, dadadam, dadadam, dadadam,

Iggy turns around, possessing all the time in
the world.

The guitar goes:

dadadam, dadadam, dadadam, dadadam,
dadadam, dadadam, dadadam, dadadam,

He is completely and utterly in control of the room,
all eyes and hearts on him.

The guitar goes:

dadadam, dadadam, dadadam, dadadam,
dadadam, dadadam, dadadam, dadadam,

He slowly, slowly raises the microphone, the audience needs some relief.

The guitar goes:

dadadam, dadadam, dadadam, dadadam,
dadadam, dadadam, dadadam, dadadam,

And finally, finally, finally:

"I AM THE PASSENGER,
AND I RIDE
AND I RIDE,
I RIDE THROUGH THE CITY AT NIGHT…"

He moves towards the front of the stage . . . and—
without giving it any thought and without looking—*he walks right off it*, right into the outstretched
hands of the audience, walks on their hands, like
Jesus on the water. That's when my tears came.

Neville Brody

It is entirely safe to say that Neville Brody is one of
the most influential graphic designers of our time.
His story begins in the U.K. music scene of the 1980s,
when he designed record covers for legendary labels
including Rocking Russian, Stiff Records, and Fetish
Records. This led to his appointment as art director of
the magazine Fetish, where he began experimenting
with a new visual language that drew upon a striking
combination of visual, architectural, and editorial
elements.

But it was his groundbreaking work as art
director for The Face magazine, from 1981 to 1986,
that allowed him to thoroughly reinvent the way in
which both designers and readers approach the idea
and expectation of what a magazine should look like.
This innovation became a much-imitated example.
The Graphic Language of Neville Brody, a monograph published in 1988, showcases that work as
well as other projects both high- and low-profile.

Based in London, Neville now operates from
the multidisciplinary design firm Research Studios.
His contemporary design oeuvre includes everything
from a redesign of the British newspaper The Times
to typefaces to an identity for Dom Pérignon.

Neville was unguarded and uncensored in our
interview. We talked about design celebrity, invented
identities, the "eternal conundrum" of the design
business, and the difficulty of doing anything truly
rebellious in today's visual culture.

*Can you tell me about the first time you remember
doing something creative?*

Well, that's really difficult. Because I was drawing
before I was walking.

Could you be a little more specific about that?

Well, no, because I have no memory of it.

*Really? So you know this because your parents told
you that you were drawing before you were walking?*

Yes, if I was walking at one or one and a half.

*So what kinds of things were you drawing? Did your
parents tell you?*

No. I've no idea whatsoever, I'm afraid. All I can say
is that from that point, there was never any doubt
as to what I was going to do. I never spent my childhood thinking, "When I'm going to grow up, I'm
going to choose a career." It was there. It was chosen
for me.

*In terms of your career, a love of drawing might have
led to a career in fine art.*

I beg to differ on that. I think I am a fine artist.

In the U.K., we do a foundation course, which
is a pregraduate course. Everyone does it here, it's
a year or two-year curriculum. It allows you to do
everything from typography to drawing to pottery
to photography. And it's a fabulous thing. So everyone does it, and they use that year to figure out what
they want to be doing.

One of the things we were taught was that
if you had something to communicate, you should
communicate to as many people as possible. I
didn't see the point in the elitist world of fine art,
where you were communicating to a narrow few.
Especially since that narrow few is self-elected.
Furthermore, the fine-art world was largely a world
of commerce. At the time, I felt very strongly that it
was a fake culture.

*Do you feel there is something more real about the
graphic design culture?*

I think that there is something more honest about
it. It is a commercial industry. And I like the idea
of trying to have something creative functioning
within a commercial industry more than I like the
notion of pretending you're in a cultural industry—when it's really all about money. Also, at that
particular time, the world of painting was a hypo-
critical one. It was limited, it was elitist, and it was
exclusive: all of the things I abhorred at the time.

*Do you still feel that the fine-art world is an elitist,
exclusive world?*

Yes, even more so now.

*When I first asked if I could interview you for this
book, you responded that I could do a book like this
without you. Why is that?*

I mean, you could. I'm sure you have some very
bright, clear-minded, inspiring people in the book.
And I'm really happy if what I've done has made
a contribution somewhere.

It is just bizarre, really. There are two
Neville Brodys: There's me, the person who gets
up in the morning and showers and gets a bus and
argues with the milkman and all of that. And there's
this other Neville Brody, which was not quite an
invention, but who came into being because I felt
I had something very strong to say in terms of
messaging. And I felt very strongly that you can't
remain on the fringe and expect to be heard. I made
a conscious attempt to use celebrity status as a
communication tool.

In what way?

To draw people to my work in order for them to get
in touch with the ideas behind it. The ideas behind
my work are quite political—with a small *p*—and
the message I convey is all about awareness. It's all

about the fact that, these days, graphic design is part of a heavily manipulative industry.

Do you feel that the work you're doing contributes to that?

Of course. Totally. We work in a commercial service, and inevitably there's compromise. It's just a question of degree.

Do you feel that the invented Neville Brody is still very much a part of who you are, or do you feel the two Nevilles are more integrated now?

I think the public-domain version hasn't been managed this year. I don't have the time. But it always astonishes me when I go to school. Every year I try and do life-drawing classes—as a student, not as a teacher—and I always find it very ironic, that I can be in an art school studying life-drawing, and in the next room there might be a design-history class studying my work.

I imagine that this is a very heady experience.

It's surreal.

When I interviewed Stefan Sagmeister, he and I talked about the idea of celebrity. He had a wonderful perspective on this. He said: "Being a famous graphic designer is like being a famous electrician."

I think Stefan's slightly wrong. In fact, he's extremely wrong. Because an electrician isn't an opinion former, but a graphic designer is. My argument is that all graphic designers hold high levels of responsibility in society. We take invisible ideas and make them tangible. That's our job. We take news or information or emotions like "hope" or "turn left" or "buy this" or "be sexy"—as well as notions of brand image as broad concepts—and we give that tangible form. We make it real for people.

Do you feel that your celebrity has impacted the
quality of your work or your approach at all?

No, not at all. We keep a very low profile as a studio. These days, my work is largely about nurturing and supporting a young team here. I don't feel that the quality or ideas have suffered. But I do think that it's harder to do radical things in media now.

In what way?

In the way that anything's possible. There was a time when anything that wasn't seen as conservative was seen as quite rebellious and radical. But these days, anything goes. You can walk down the street naked in the middle of London, and no one would bat an eyelid. You can buy hardcore porn anywhere, and no one bats an eyelid. It's no longer an issue. You can choose any font, use it in any way, and it's all good. There's no reason why one is more worthy than any other. There's no shock value anymore.

Then how do you think messages best get through
to people?

The problem is that there is a mediocrity born of generic culture right now. Any city you go to looks the same. I travel a lot. And whether I wake up in a hotel in Singapore or Toronto, the experience is the same, the culture is the same. Even the pictures on the wall are the same. And they are the same pictures I might find at the front of the British Airways cabin on the flight over. It's all interchangeable. This signifies that a core meaning has gotten lost somehow.

But the generation I'm part of thought the work we do could help make society a better place. And that ended. Reagan and Thatcher destroyed that. They believed that culture is not about identity, but rather is about coding, which can be then exploited for advertising use. It turned everything upside down. In the U.K., it even turned colleges into financial institutions.

Do you feel that you can make a difference with your work now?

What I love about this business is that it's an eternal conundrum—an eternal paradox. If you're working in the commercial world, how do you work for the benefit of people? Commercial work largely means that you're being commissioned. And this means that you've been commissioned by someone who wants to benefit from that commissioning, and 99 percent of the time, it's for financial gain.

And how do you navigate through that?

You have to look for opportunities. The problem right now is that radical design is just a fashionable space. There's nothing really radical out there. Radical, for instance, would be non-commercial.

Do you feel like people don't pay attention unless they're shocked?

I think people have become immune.

How do you reach people now? Have you thought about how things stand out?

Yes. A non-commercial space. A space devoid of advertising would be a shock.

How do you know when something you've created is good?

The work that I try and achieve, and the kind of work I've always tried to achieve, has a high degree of invested ambiguity.

What does that mean?

In the advertising business, it's not in the interest of advertisers for people to think about what they're presented with. It's in the interest of advertisers that people choose to think in the way the advertisers intend them to. It's a formulaic thing, where there's only one possible outcome in advertising. That creates a space where the "right to thought" is taken away from people.

I've always tried to approach my work as being open-ended and with a degree of abstraction or ambiguity. This prevents it from being a mono-logue, because it is a dialogue. The work is only completed when a viewer has looked at it and made his or her own decision as to the full meaning of the piece.

How do your clients respond to that intentional ambiguity?

You can't always do it. There are clients who resist it. We've done branding exercises where things have ended up very fixed. And that is part and parcel of working in the commercial design industry.

What do you think are the long-term ramifications of that for designers?

Well, it's a gloriously healthy industry. And it looks beautiful these days. My biggest obsession at the moment is that nothing is difficult.

Tell me what you mean by "difficult."

I don't mean "difficult" as in raising a child is dif-ficult, or keeping a dog is difficult. We've gone into a realm of fear wherein we try to make things as easy as possible. **No one's prepared to engage with difficult ideas anymore. It is very rare that graphic design is a difficult, engaging space these days.**

Even fine art is not difficult anymore. It's sensation-alist, but it's not difficult.

When do you think the last moment of "difficulty" was?

I think some of Stefan's work is difficult. I think some of Tibor's work was difficult, but highly enter-taining. And then you have to go back awhile. In terms of fine art in the U.K., we've had a "Brit Art" thing going on, a pop-art thing. It's all been very sensationalist. It's what I call post-production art.

What does that mean?

Basically, you start with a sensation you want to achieve, and then work backwards and plot how to achieve it—in the same way that advertising does. It's exactly the same. Art these days is like an advertising industry. The point is:

There is nothing really different. There's nothing really dangerous, there's nothing really difficult out there right now. And I think we need some things to start galvanizing people. I think we need things that allow people to think in non-commercial ways.

Do you feel that you had any failures in your career?

Oh, totally. One of my biggest failures was *The Face* magazine.

How do you see that as a failure?

Well, the whole message of *The Face* was that you don't have to accept conditioned rules. You can go out and challenge things and create new spaces and new expression.

How would you view this as a failure?

Well, the failure was that people copied it, if you see what I mean.

Did they copy it, or were they trying to—

No, they copied it, especially in the U.K. It became a copycat culture here.

But how do you see that as a failure?

Because people missed the message, they just took the stylistic attributes. And it wasn't about stylistic attributes. It was about the idea that language is organic, that language can evolve as society evolves.

It should be individual, and it shouldn't be in the control of the few. It should be a constant, living process—not a dead thing, which is what we've been taught at college.

So do you see that as a failure of the work that you did, or do you see that as a failure in the way that society—

I'd say it was just a personal failure, and that I misjudged it. *The Face* was an open laboratory, really. And each issue of *The Face* was the result of another month's experimentations. And none of these were supposed to be fixed points; they were all supposed to be evolutionary.

Why do you think it became so copied?

Because at the time, there wasn't anything else out there like it.

Really? Do you think that's the only reason?

No, what happened was also because it was new.

But there are a lot of new things that don't speak to people to the extent that they want to copy the design, or to use it to express themselves.

Maybe. My problem is I can't seem to distance myself from what I perceive to be a failure. This is why I did *Arena* magazine afterwards, in which nothing changed. When I was at *The Face*, there were only a few of us, and we worked late at night; but it was not a massive movement of any kind. Nevertheless, there was a distinct pressure of expectation that everything should be new all the time. So new became our norm. People expected things to be new. When we did an issue that was similar to the previous month's issue, we were criticized for it. And I ended up feeling that the only way to react was to do something that never changed.

And do you feel that was more successful?

Well, in the end, it became something else. When

I started up in design, I was in this manic search for the new. This desperate search for the new was a futile process. This was my attempt to sit down and take stock. I see *Arena* more as a park bench than as a magazine. It was time to take stock, check my shoes, buy nice clothes, live comfortably for a while, and see the world again. And then, of course, I couldn't sit still, and we tried to make Helvetica seem emotional, which is why some of the later work was much more expressive.

At the end of the day, I think we must always try to expand our spectrum. The more people we try to communicate with, the more generic our messages have to become. And as our messages become more generic, it's less likely that people will have access to anything that's different. I know this is slightly negative, but it's not meant to be. It's a plea for humanism.

Peter Saville

For as long as I can remember, I have had an intense fascination with record covers. The albums of the rock band Yes, featuring ethereal, otherworldly illustrations by Roger Dean, first entranced me.

But my world was permanently transformed when I fell under the spell of Peter Saville's work for Joy Division. I studied the cover art with the precision of a biologist, and the more I looked, the more I found. This, to me, is part of the magnificence of Saville's creations. While often minimalist and nearly always postmodern, they are layered with abundant nuance and boast a magical attention to detail.

In addition to his record covers for Joy Division, New Order, Suede, and Pulp, Peter has also created a substantial body of work for an endless list of über-fabulous fashion designers, most notably Jil Sander, Yohji Yamamoto, and Stella McCartney. He has even created a brand identity for the supermodel Kate Moss.

In 2003, Peter published the monograph Designed by Peter Saville, *a gorgeous tome that was a partner piece to a major retrospective of his work at London's Design Museum. In 2004, he was anointed the first-ever creative director of the city of Manchester in England.*

Peter and I had a long, sprawling conversation about the lack of intellectual rigor in cult-pop design, his controversial sojourn at Pentagram, and why, six years into his career, he didn't know how to design a letterhead.

[Saville begins without prompting...]

Before we get started, one relevant thing to state is that I believe that communication design is *for* others and *to* others. This is an important thing for younger or would-be graphic designers to recognize.

Can you elaborate?

Younger designers and would-be designers must understand that communication design is for others and to others.

As opposed to—

For yourself, to yourself. **There is a great misconception in this era of graphic design that it is a medium of self-expression.**

Why do you think that misconception exists?

Partly because of work by people such as myself.

Why is that? In what way?

It may not be evident in the U.S. yet, but it will be. It is very evident in the U.K., especially among design graduates of the past few years. The forms of communications arts which have been the most "directional," especially to young people in formative years—such as fashion campaigns, editorial design to some extent, and the record cover in particular—are very persuasive mediums to young people. They arrive at a very formative time in their life, and in the context of a kind of obsessive association.

In particular, young men are obsessive about certain aspects of music—especially of the cult aspects of music—and they tend to embrace everything that comes with it. So if you're a Marilyn Manson fan, you take on the entire package. If you're into rap, you take on the entire package. This is what adolescents do. The graphic arts associated with pop culture are the entry-level doorway into this discipline.

And they're actually quite misleading or misguiding from the point of view of the profession of communication design. Cult pop is a free-form zone of autonomous expression for the designer. There is very little or no discipline involved. For the last 20 years or so, it has been acting as an "entry-level art" for young people, enticing them into the profession.

Why do you think there is no discipline involved in cult-pop design?

Because there *is* no discipline involved. Because none of it really matters. The imagery to do with pop culture is irrelevant.

So there's no rigor in it?

There's certainly no intellectual rigor in it. And there's no business or commercial rigor in it. Twenty-two-year-olds design record covers for other twenty-two-year-olds. The music industry makes money out of it. I have never, ever, ever—in all the years I did record covers—I never had what we would call a business or positioning discussion vis-à-vis a record cover.

And still, to this day, you don't?

No. Not in the way we would experience in the broader aspects of business. It's entirely emotion-ally led. I mean, what do we think the brief is for a Madonna cover? There is only one brief: Keep Madonna happy. That's it. Madonna has to be happy. That's the brief. Because a Madonna album is going to sell. It doesn't matter if the package is a brown paper bag. It will sell. The biggest hurdle here is whether the talent is happy.

You blame yourself for this lack of discipline?

No, not the general lack of discipline. This started

before my time. It's just the way that pop culture works. Lately, I've had one or two clients in the skateboarding and snowboarding business, what I would consider the cult end of fashion. It's all the same thing; it's all entirely intuitive. That's why you get young people to design it. They do a cover that they like, and quid pro quo, their peer group likes it. That's it.

It is all an entirely intuitive experience; consequently, it's not worth very much money. You don't get paid more as you become more experienced or more professional or better at what you do. There's a budget for doing a record cover whether you're 20 or 50, and that's all there is to it.

Do you think that as we age, we become less intuitive?

No. We just become less intuitive to that popculture sphere. We become intuitive to another sphere. In my opinion, designing record covers is not an appropriate job for a 40-year-old or even a 30-year-old. What is tricky is that this area of pop culture has been offering a doorway to graphics for young people. But it's a very misleading introduction to the profession itself. Let's face it: There are very few 18-year-olds starting off at an art college who really want to go there because they love the new BP logo. That's the key.

I think that classes in the graphic arts are really entry-level fine art—in the same way that pop art is entry-level art for the uneducated and the uncultured.

Why do you think it's entry-level fine art?

Because it's dumbed down. These days, the graphic arts are basically taking their cues from contemporary fine art.

For example?

In the previous decade, they took their cues from fashion. In the decade before that, they took it from pop art maybe. But the last decade is increasingly about contemporary fine art becoming the lead discipline. It's disseminated broadly, it's in the media: Art is the new fashion, blah blah blah. And of course, young people are taking their lead from it. They're interested in it. You know, Jeff Koons is not all that difficult to get, superficially.

How did you get started in graphic design?

I got into graphic design because of my high school art teacher. Along with my best friend Malcolm Garrett, I was talking to this teacher about the future, and he asked us if we had ever considered graphic design. And we said, "No, what's that?" This was 1974. He explained to us that being a graphic designer was actually a profession. It was hard to believe that what we liked doing during lunchtime at school was something we could do for a living—and this was very exciting for us.

Then we went off to college and got the very dull introduction to the fact that design is actually difficult. We were introduced to the discipline of design in the '70s. But—our big "but"—was this: Whilst we were at college, something fundamentally radical happened in pop culture. Pop culture was briefly taken back by young people. Punk rock seized the wheel of pop culture from business and gave it to the people and to the kids themselves. This lasted for about ten minutes.

So it was sort of the perfect storm for you to be able to do what you wanted.

Yes. By the mid-'70s, pop culture had become an entirely commoditized dimension of business. You went to see concerts with 3,000 other people, and you dutifully bought the products of major record labels. There was nothing personal in it at all; it was business.

Then punk stepped in, and all sorts of independent record labels sprung up. And this happened at exactly the time I graduated from college. So I became a joint founder of a record label in Manchester. Immediately, I found myself with a group of people who were entirely non-business, and I was both client and designer. Nobody at Factory Records had anything to do with business. It wasn't even a company; it wasn't a job for anybody. It was a group of people who thought they'd like to do things differently. No money was involved, and so everybody did exactly as they wanted out of complete naïveté.

So I did the record covers that I would have liked to receive myself. I did what I would have liked to find in the record shop. It was even more extreme in my position at Factory: The groups themselves were not involved. They actually delegated all design decisions to me. With all the other groups I've ever worked with, it's been a different type of situation. You are acting as the art director or designer of a client who happens to be Jarvis Cocker or Madonna or whomever. It is a professional playground.

Whereas when I was working with Factory, the groups stepped out of the visual decision-making process, and they left the design up to me. I had a 14-year period during which I had an unsupervised platform that reached an increasingly large international audience. With groups such as Joy Division and New Order, I had a direct line to at least 150,000 people for whatever I wanted to do. I had no given creative brief. I had no gatekeeper. And this—partly because of what I did, but much more because of the context of Joy Division and New Order, and the medium—this brokered an enormous amount of influence.

I still can't quite believe how great a responsibility this level of influence was. But it was enormous. There are a vast number of people who tell me they became graphic designers because of my record slips.

How does that make you feel?

Well, I have to say, "I'm sorry." I apologize. I usually say, "I'm sorry about that," and they smile knowingly. Because it's not like that anymore. You do not do what you want to do. And yet, this notion is rather prevalent. It's prevalent in design education at the moment.

In what way?

It's rather dangerous. There are a lot of self-initiated briefs going on in design education. And this is helpful to the individual who wants to look deep and ask questions about where they want to be. But that discovery has to be structured within the context of business. It's not art. Graphic design is a dangerous term now. We should really call it communications design, because graphic design doesn't really mean anything. What is the job? The job is communications design, and that is conveying somebody else's message to a prescribed audience. Who you are and what you think about it doesn't necessarily come into play. The job is to articulate the message from A to B.

Now this is very different to the professional thinking that we might associate with the graphic design greats of, let's say, the '70s.

For example?

Milton Glaser, Saul Bass, Massimo Vignelli. Certainly the Pentagram founders. They did have a style, but they were working in the intellectual and philosophical dimension of the practice. There was a discipline to how they communicated to people. They were acting professionally on behalf of their clients. They were strategists, not hired killers. And when we think about the profession of graphic design—the grown-up, mature profession of graphic design—it *is* about intellect and strategy. It's about how we might best communicate the needs of A to audience B.

*When did your transformation occur? You started out
in a way that you felt was entirely intuitive, and now
you have radically different ideas about what you do.*

I had a channel that allowed me to do what I wanted
to do, which did broker enormous influence. Of
course, within a year or so, as soon as I moved from
Manchester to London and actually started to work
professionally—certainly by the mid-'80s (as soon as
I made the step out of the music industry, out of the
sort of the "children's land")—then I was confronted
with the reality of communications design.

Was it traumatic for you?

It was traumatic in the sense that it took us about
a year to do a letterhead.

What do you mean?

By 1985, I had three D&AD Silver awards, but I
couldn't do a letterhead. As much as I was flattered
by the request to do a letterhead and identity for
a gallery, I realized that I had no idea what I was
doing. I realized that I may be successful as a record
company designer—and people may pay us lots of
money for that—but for this, I would have to go back
to the beginning. I had to start from nothing and
learn from the ground up. The same thing happened
six months later, with a fashion project. I didn't
know how to do it.

*Looking back at the work that you did prior to that,
how do you feel about it now, looking at it from a more
critical perspective?*

I see it as art practice in the context of a playground.
The New Order covers were closer to art practice,
but with none of the intellectual rigor and discipline
that a fine-art course would have imposed upon me.
The rest is children's art.

*Is there anything you regret about the work that you
did at the time?*

Not really. Some of it is better than the rest. Some of it is still amongst my favorite work of all time. Some of it is fantastic.

What do you think is the best of it?

The cover for a New Order album in 1983 called *Power, Corruption & Lies*—and its attendant single "Blue Monday"—are very interesting, and are reasonably interesting as art practice. They were of great significance to other younger people who became designers, who became artists, fashion designers, photographers, product designers, etc. The influence brokered upon a younger generation of artists—of fine artists—was immense. That's the sort of interesting thing about 14- to 18-year-olds: They are not yet doctors, lawyers, artists, or architects. That level of influence was completely across the board.

There are now several generations of artists who quote those covers as their formative influences. Similarly, I meet architects who are fans, fashion designers who are fans, photographers who are fans, endless graphic designers who are fans.

Currently, I am working with the Manchester City Council, and I have met [council members] who are fans. These are people who work in the public sector but bought my records when they were younger. I'm creative director of the City of Manchester now, and that's directly linkable back to that early work.

How do you know when the work you're doing is good?

It's kind of interesting, that one. You know when you've solved the problem. From 1985 until now, I've struggled to operate within the real context of communications design. I don't actually enjoy it. It isn't really what I want to do. I am more interested in my own opinions. So, I gradually have fostered a gallery opportunity. But I'm being very, very careful about it, because it's a slippery slope.

My day job in the meantime—for the last 20
years—has been the activity and environment of
work for others. And fortunately, I've gotten better
at doing it. I had two years at Pentagram in London,
which was invaluable. Really, really invaluable.

In what way?

I got to learn something from my elders—and I
could say "betters"—but really from my elders. I
learned enormous amounts. That's the thing about
being a partner at Pentagram: You are temporarily
put on a platform with the other guys. And I had
never worked for anybody. I'd never had the benefit
of a mentor. So, suddenly I had 15 of them. And
they were some of the best people in the western
world in the profession of graphic design: John
McConnell, David Hillman, Colin Forbes, and Alan
Fletcher. You couldn't help but learn. I mean, John
McConnell, David Hillman, Alan, Colin—I learned
an enormous amount from them. I learned things
every day. I mean, I upset them and I frustrated
them, and in the end, they asked me to go. But in the
two years I was with them, I learned an enormous
amount from the collective wisdom of Pentagram.

Did you want to leave?

Yes, I had thought about it, and I had to leave. We
were not compatible. But in my opinion, it probably
would have been better for Pentagram if I did stay.

Why?

I believed that the incompatibility was symptomatic
of an issue that Pentagram needed to face out.

Which was?

I was a kind of fly in the ointment. I was part of a
generational shift. Yet I actually believed in the
philosophical structure of Pentagram. I believed in
the opportunity that Pentagram provided for the
individual to be effective within the wider terms

of business. After all, a single person doing British Airways doesn't work. The kind of Paul Rand and IBM relationship doesn't happen any more. Big businesses need big companies to talk to. And yet, it's usually the talent or the vision of one person that defines the work. But it's very difficult to become a contender for that kind of large-scale project.

The Pentagram structure did that. It actually created a situation where one person could interact with the problem. The problem usually is that once you've built up a 60- or 100-person-strong company to be a potential service, you've become a business-person. You are no longer a designer. That activity disappeared years and years ago. It is what always happens. It's the classic pyramid structure of creative companies. It doesn't work.

Pentagram was this brilliant alternative that Colin and Alan and company came up with in the early '70s. It was a brilliant idea. And I believed in it totally. I just didn't believe in the look. I believed in the essence of it—as a solution to a problem—but not in the look. My reservation about Pentagram was that it was glued to the look of its founding era. I believed that they didn't really understand fashion, and they didn't really understand the kind of fast-moving character of pop.

Do you still feel that way?

Yeah, I think that it is a handicap. Pentagram was a supergroup founded out of five of the biggest, most radical names in the later 1960s. That's what made it Pentagram. You've got to complement like with like—especially when you experience generational passages of time. To a certain extent, in the '90s, Pentagram needed the next radical generation. Whether they liked it or not, they needed it. And I was a representative of that generation. But it was just all too difficult for them.

The sort of weird realization I got at Penta-gram—once I was in—was that they really wanted me to recant and see that they were the one true church: "The fact that he's joined our club is an acknowledgment that we are, after all, correct." And I was like, "Oh shit. I thought we were going to change it. I thought you had the will to change it." That was why I joined.

So how do you keep yourself continually changing?

Well, this question probably gets to the essence of what you need to ask me: what my work is about. My work is about my opinion of what I see around me.

That's flying in the face of what you started by saying—but is that how you started your career?

It was the same then. My work then was about what I saw around me. My opinion of the world around me, and what I felt it needed. And that's what informed my work at the beginning. Factory allowed me a completely free rein to express that. Whenever I had to work professionally, I found that people didn't really understand what I was talking about. They always did later, but they never did at the beginning. Usually other people stepped in and profited from what I had done earlier.

In what way?

Everything I did in the '80s got copied for the High Street.* I don't want to sound too arrogant about this, but along with one or two other people, the communications world of the past 20 years looks how I thought it should look.

In what regard?

There's a clarity of precision, a kind of quotation within the context of fashion, of what we might call "lifestyle." A communication through other visual codes, through semiotics. This is where I was at

* A British term for the street where all the major shops are located.

odds with the Pentagram crew. The '60s and '70s produced a type of communication through visual pun. The New York school—when executed by its best practitioners, and in the early stages of cultural awareness—was very effective. I see the period since the '50s as a period of postwar, sociocultural democratization. I see the last 50 or 60 years as a period during which ordinary people have been introduced to culture. Culture has been democratized over the last 50 or 60 years.

How has culture been democratized?

Ordinary people now have a choice of furniture, of architectural styles, of clothing, of fashion, of food. Ordinary people didn't have that before. The U.S. is a special example of what you call "the American dream." In truth, the American dream doesn't really become commoditized until midcentury.

How do you feel about that commoditization?

It's essential. It has a downside, but it's essential. Our choices as ordinary people now—these are choices previous generations didn't have. Our lifestyles now are a kind of cheap version of what was formerly privilege.

By the time I was at art college in the latter half of the '70s, I could say everything I wanted with the difference between Helvetica and Futura. Say everything! I can transcend 20 years with those two fonts.

I don't wish to communicate to everybody. Very few things are for everybody. If you don't understand my communication, that's fine, because it's probably not for you. But the ones who do understand are the ones that it's for. So the late '70s are the beginning—the early stages—of what we understand as designer culture and lifestyle culture.

Now, that is still the predominant methodology in communications design. And my era brings that in. And I was gravely at odds with my tutors at college, who rejected it. And I was gravely at odds ten years later with the old guys at Pentagram, who just didn't get it. They didn't see this methodology as design. They couldn't see, you know, because it upset their beloved idea. They couldn't see it. And these were the new codes of communications design that are now ubiquitous.

Do you feel like your older work is as relevant now as when you created it?

Well, people seem to think it is. I think it's more relevant in its attitudes than in its forms. After all, it's 25 years ago.

The only work that I can do now that's relevant is the work I would put into a gallery. Or when I occasionally have a free-form project.

I think everybody feels that the work you were doing when you first started out in your career was very much an influence for the times and the ensuing years. And you just said now that the only work you could conceive to be relevant was—

Self-expression, yes, self-expression.

So how could you conceivably do relevant graphic design?

I don't think you can.

Do you think anybody can?

When you're working for the public sector. As creative director of a city, I find the process incredibly, incredibly difficult, and not particularly exciting. A day in Manchester town hall is not quite the same as, you know, backstage at a Jil Sander show.

How do you feel about the fact that design is now being used as advertising?

This is where a dilemma and crisis come in. I believe that good design is fundamentally orientated around truth, and once it loses its truth, you've lost it completely. The semiotics of good design imply that if we've redesigned a magazine or a hotel or a hospital, it is now better; that new problems have been solved; that new challenges have been addressed. In contemporary projects, we're often not making things better, we're just making things different: "It's just different because we'd like you to buy more." It's just decoration. Design is losing its essential values because it's being used for the wrong purposes. It's being used to sell us stuff. It's being used as advertising.

I was proud and happy to do fashion in the '80s when I felt that fashion was something still being disseminated to people. But now it's like a drug. Now it's like an addiction. You do not need a new handbag every season. You just don't. And they're all rubbish. You just don't need them.

So what do we do? How do we change this?

The big problem for communications designers is they have to earn a living. And this is the new job. We've become messenger boys. We do the handwriting for these people. I likened it recently to pop culture: It's gone from being like acid to being like crack. Pop culture is like crack. It doesn't give you anything. It just wants to take your money, and when you've run out, you can fuck off. And unfortunately, the graphic design community has become the lecherous boys of this business. It's a big problem.

You can choose to do something different. If you say, I'm going to make my own poster, then you're a politician, or a writer, or an artist. You can say, "Fuck it, I'm going to do my own book." Well, you'd better write it first. The problem with graphic design is it's the interface. You can change what you're saying to people, but then you become something else. Graphics is just the interface. And this is the problem. The work is the work.

You're not feeling very optimistic about it.

No, I'm not. That's pretty much why I've retired it. Because there's lots of beautiful work going on, but what is it for? What is it for? You've got this new problem, and it's something that can be dealt with, but not with a frigging 5,000 more graphic designers every year. I believe you must question whether or not you identify with the need you are articulating. You should ask yourself, "Am I doing something that is embarrassing?"

If you go around feeling embarrassed, it's a very good signal. And you know when it feels right, and when it feels embarrassing. And this is a big, big problem for graphic designers. Because we are being asked to legitimize commerce.

The very essence of what I am trying to say is this: We must be communicators of the world. We help other people see things. This is at the heart of what we do. And of course, where you do that and how you do that must stay apace with your own life and evolution. I mean, I'm 51 years of age now! People still phone and ask me if I want to design album covers. They tell me I can do whatever I want, but it's very difficult for me to explain that the rack of a record store is not where I wish to express myself. Go ask a 20-year-old.

For me, it's really important to stay within the terms of your own relevance—which means don't be permanently 18. Shift your point of engagement to that which is relative to you. Try to find work that has meaning. You have to help invest meaning into the work. And it is very difficult to invest meaning in something that doesn't have meaning to you. And that really is the key:

You've got to like what you're doing, and then you do it well. You've got to like what you're doing, and you have to put meaning into it for others.

Emily Oberman &
Bonnie Siegler /
Number 17

The first time I met Emily Oberman and Bonnie Siegler was in 1999. I had been a devoted admirer of their work for as long as I could remember, so I invited them to speak at a conference I was organizing. Remarkably, they agreed.

Emily and Bonnie are best friends and partners in Number 17, a design firm creating work for television, film, print, and the Web. But they are also individually known for influential work they created prior to starting their firm; most notably Emily's collaborations with Tibor Kalman at the legendary design firm M&Co and Bonnie's breakthrough designs at VH1. So when I first met them, I was struck by their age. How could such fresh-faced women be so accomplished and so young? The answer is easy: by the sheer force of their unique talent.

These witty, stylish women are the brains behind the newly reinvigorated Colors *magazine, spots for Nickelodeon and MTV, the opening titles for* Saturday Night Live, *and the design for* Lucky *magazine, to name just a few standouts.*

I talked with the duo in their TriBeCa studio, an environment showcasing unusual collections that include every paper phone message they have received. But most dazzling was their rapport: It was palpable. They joyfully finished each other's sentences and interrupted each other as Bonnie talked about designing her Bat Mitzvah invitation and Emily shared a list of things she loves.

When was the last fight you had?

EMILY. It was today.

What did you fight about?

EMILY. Whether to meet with you or not.

What happened? Where was the fight?

BONNIE. On the street.

EMILY. Bonnie asked if we could move our meeting
with you to Friday, and I said no. And then she
said, "Why not?" and I explained why not.

BONNIE. In a very angry way.

EMILY. It was such a married-couple fight. It had
nothing to do with a project or with creativity.

BONNIE. We were already late for a meeting, and
we were coming from another meeting, and we
had too much to do, and...

EMILY. That's what it was. The kids were driving
us crazy!

So was the fight resolved?

BONNIE. Yes. We went into the meeting, we both had
good ideas and that was that. Over.

*You didn't have to analyze what went wrong, check
to see if everything was okay; make sure you still love
each other?*

BONNIE. No.

EMILY. No.

*What happens when you have a creative
disagreement?*

BONNIE. We have very heated discussions when we
don't agree creatively, when one of us likes one
thing and one of us likes something else.

EMILY. If we're working on something, and we come
up with ideas but prefer different solutions, they
will both go to the client. But if one of us wouldn't
be happy if that direction moves forward, then we
have a conflict.

BONNIE. If one of us feels *that* strongly about not doing something and one of us feels strongly about doing it, things can get pretty heated.

EMILY. We have a rule: If one of us feels strongly against something, it won't go forward. This ensures that nothing comes out of the office that we hate. Neither one of us can hate anything that comes out of here.

BONNIE. There is also a fine line between dislike and "dislike strongly enough" to have a fight about.

EMILY. Right.

What made you decide to have a partnership as opposed to going out on your own individually?

EMILY. It is too hard. I wouldn't be able to do it on my own. Design is really hard to do alone.

BONNIE. Also, when we started Number 17, we were 22.

Who made the first overture to start a partnership?

BONNIE. We talked about it from...

EMILY. From day one...

BONNIE. From the first day we met.

Was it love at first sight?

BONNIE. Yes. We went out to lunch, at Cozy Burger, and talked about starting our own business three hours after we met.

How much compromise do you feel is involved in your day-to-day relationship?

EMILY. I was just talking to my husband, Paul Sahre, about this. Paul is Mr. Lone Wolf. He doesn't know how we do "this." Bonnie and I both have egos. We both have big ideas. I guess there is a fair amount of compromise involved in our partnership, but I don't mind. When Bonnie and I truly collaborate, perhaps I'll have the idea, and she does the design, and then I add another piece of text, and she adds an image.

When we toss things back and forth, there is no compromise at all. That is when it's magic.

Now this is not the way we work on every project. Some projects reflect one of us more than the other.

BONNIE. But it's definitely the best when we play together. Instead of one of us looking over the other's shoulder...

EMILY. ...which I also love for a different reason. When one of us is the designer and the other is the art director, or when one of us is working more closely on a project with one of the other designers in the office, that can be wonderful as well.

BONNIE. But the flip side of compromise is when you have a blank page and you have no idea what to put on it. Or perhaps something is there, but you can't take it any further or you've looked at it too long, and you're stuck. At those times, you have someone—someone who is not working for you, but is a partner with you and a better version of yourself—to hand it off to. So, yes, sometimes you have to compromise a bit, but the benefits far outweigh the compromises.

EMILY. I love not having to go into a meeting or a lecture alone. I love that if I forget my lines, Bonnie is there to pick them up; or if I'm fumbling in a meeting, Bonnie can say something to distract them.

BONNIE. A "Hey, look over there!" thing.

In a lot of design studio partnerships, it's rare for the partnership to be two designers.

EMILY. Yes.

It's also rare for the partnership to be two designers who clearly consider the other to be a better version of herself.

BONNIE. I think that can be attributed to the female– female dynamic. Men are more egomaniacal in

this arrangement, and women are more insecure.
In the male partnerships we know, the conflict is
about one of them feeling that he does more work,
while the other partner is not holding his weight.
With us, it's the opposite.

EMILY. Our biggest fights tend to be when one of
us feels like we're not pulling our own weight!
I will think, "Oh my God, Bonnie is doing everything, I am doing nothing, I am fucking up so
badly, I have got to do better." I never think,
"Oh my God, Bonnie is fucking up, so I've got
to do more." I never think that way.

I find that in many relationships, whether they are
love relationships or business partnerships, there is
one person who does this *and the person who does* that.
As long as you're the person that is the sole owner of
that, *and nobody encroaches in your territory, there*
seems to be a lot more success.

BONNIE. I think we have a certain amount of that.

EMILY. I do too.

BONNIE. We each own a different part of the brain.

Which part of the brain do each of you own?

BONNIE. I am definitely more logical. I handle more
of the business issues, which I enjoy. I actually like
the business side of the business. It's easy for me,
and it uses a different part of my brain.

EMILY. I am the opposite of whatever logical is.

BONNIE. Abstract.

EMILY. I am also the one who is more out there in
the design community, talking to people. I think
I'm more comfortable talking on stage than
Bonnie is. I think that I'm more extroverted.

BONNIE. Definitely, definitely, definitely.

How comfortable and confident are you in your own
personal judgments?

EMILY. Bonnie is pretty comfortable in her own
judgment.

BONNIE. I am.

EMILY. And I am less confident. I am this very weird blend, which is annoying…

BONNIE. So you can imagine how it is to me.

EMILY. I have this huge ego, and I am incredibly insecure at the same time. Bonnie's confidence is daunting.

In what way?

BONNIE. I don't know what it is. Here, in the office, I don't have a rearview mirror. We send in work, and I don't look back.

EMILY. She has no regrets. She regrets nothing.

BONNIE. But at home, with my family, my rearview mirror is one of those extra giant ones.

You differentiate?

BONNIE. Oh yes.

EMILY. Bonnie's insecurities make her seem more confident.

How?

BONNIE. I don't know, but I'll try and explain it. Emily can very easily admit if she's afraid that she may not look good in something she's wearing. That is a very easy thing for her to say. I also can feel that I don't look good in something, but I feel soooo bad about it that I won't be able to admit it. So even though the emotion is identical, the behavior is not. I would be too insecure to articulate how I feel.

So it comes off as confidence?

BONNIE. Perhaps. But very often that's simply not the case.

How do you know when you've created a design that's good?

BONNIE. It's the dumb-ass idea.

The dumb-ass idea?

> BONNIE. It's the idea that's so obvious; it's the idea that's been sitting there all along. It's just there: Waiting for us to pluck it out of the air.

How do you pluck things out of the air? How do they come to you?

> BONNIE. We pluck them out of the air.

How do you find ideas? How do they magically appear?

> BONNIE. We are people first and designers second. We are lucky in that most of our clients come to us for "us."
>
> EMILY. We are the audience for most of our clients.
>
> BONNIE. Oftentimes, we are the audience, and we know how we would like to be spoken to. This helps, though it's not a prerequisite.
>
> EMILY. But you're not answering the question.
>
> BONNIE. What *is* the question?
>
> EMILY. Can *anyone* answer this question? Sometimes it happens in a flash, and sometimes you work and work and really dwell on things, and suddenly, you have a forest-through-the-trees type of experience. You work and work, and you can't see the forest through the trees, and you go crazy, and then suddenly, flash! There is the forest through the trees.
>
> BONNIE. We also include content in our design thinking. In presenting our design solutions, we come up with ideas for content. We always do that. Always. It's part of the way we think.
>
> EMILY. We still do what the client has asked for, but we will always present the idea we think the client should go with as well.

You said that most of your clients come to you for "you," and that you are the audience. But you've been together now for 14 years, so "you as you" has changed. Has your type of client changed? Are they 14 years older?

> EMILY. No, not really.

So perhaps you're known for doing a certain kind of work?

> BONNIE. The type of work we do is very broad. We design books, we design hotels, and we do a lot of work in television.

So are your clients coming to you because you're their audience, or are they coming to you because you're good at what you do?

> EMILY. Perhaps they're coming to us because of the way that we think and how we're able to fully relate to an audience—their audience—in the broadest possible sense.

When did you both know that you wanted to be graphic designers?

> EMILY. I always say that I went into the family business. My father was a graphic designer; my mother was a painter and an illustrator. There was always typography around me. There were always photographs. All of my parents' friends were graphic designers or photographers or illustrators. Now, my parents are pleased as punch because I'm the only one out of all their friends—out of all the kids of their friends—who doesn't need to explain what I do. Because they all know. So they are very, very happy.

Bonnie, What about you? When did you discover that you wanted to be a graphic designer?

> BONNIE. We should have answered each other's questions, because I knew your answer, and I'm sure that you know mine.
>
> BONNIE. [To Emily] Which answer do you think I'm going to say?
>
> EMILY. *Little Blue and Little Yellow?*

What are little blue and little yellow?

> BONNIE. It's a children's book. By Leo Lionni. I can't

even tell you why, but as a six-year-old, I was obsessed with it. It did something to me. I had never seen anything like it, and I still love it. Because of that book, I designed my own Bat Mitzvah invitation, even though I didn't know what I was doing. I had to.

Do you still have the invitation? Why did you want to design it?

BONNIE. I still have it. It was just something that I had to do, I'm not sure why. I had gotten other Bat Mitzvah invitations, and when I saw them, I knew I had to design one, but I didn't know there was a profession called "graphic design." I didn't know anything. And then, in high school, I discovered Andy Warhol. And I became obsessed with him. And then, as I read about Andy Warhol, I slowly learned there was a profession called graphic design. It seemed to fit all my weird interests.

For example?

BONNIE. When I went on family trips, I was obsessed with all the hotel amenities, and I had no idea why. I slowly learned about what seemed like a fetish and realized there was a name for it. It was graphic design! It took years, but once I knew, that was it.

As designers, what are you afraid of?

[*Silence.*]

BONNIE. Are you waiting for me to answer?

EMILY. She just did.

[*Laughter.*]

BONNIE. I have an answer. My greatest fear is that someone will realize that they shouldn't be paying attention to that woman behind the curtain. My greatest fear is that someone will realize that I'm a sham. I think this is one of the things that keeps me working. Oh! And flying. I am afraid of flying.

What do you love most about graphic design?

> BONNIE. Everything. Graphic design allows me to use every part of my brain. I couldn't do anything else.

How do you use every part of your brain?

> BONNIE. As designers, we get to do the analysis and the problem-solving. We get to take a blank piece of paper and transform it into something else. Something magical. We get to work with interesting clients. We use our management skills and interpersonal relationship skills and math skills. Everything.
>
> EMILY. I love it when we get to put our talent to good use, and when we get to work on something that changes how people think. I love it when we get to work on something that helps people. I love when we get to use our skills in order to help change the world. One other thing: I love that with every new project we undertake, we learn something. We learn something new every day. How lucky is that?

James Victore

The first time I saw James Victore, he was wearing a gorilla suit. And no, he wasn't trick-or-treating. He was headlining a talk for the New York chapter of the AIGA, the professional association for design. Titled "Mad As Hell," the presentation was classic Victore: brash, brilliant, and unbridled. Victore didn't focus on his impressive client roster or his singular talent, but rather crafted a presentation that discussed the designer as a master communicator who had an obligation to inspire social change.

The second time I saw Victore, he and Caroline Kennedy Schlossberg were speaking at an event for students involved in an AIGA mentorship program. Unfettered by conventional norms, James addressed the students with raw honesty, enthusiasm, and quite a few expletives. In fact, I remember that one AIGA staffer kept track of the number of times James used the word "fuck," as she planned an exit strategy from her job. She needn't have worried. Not only did the students give Victore a standing ovation, they spent hours after the event clamoring for the signed posters he was giving out.

James is a master designer with a kind, generous, and engaging spirit. The day we met, he picked me up on his motorcycle for a trip to his studio. We spent the rest of the afternoon talking about the responsibility of designers in today's world, creative freedom, and his parents' disappointment that their son didn't become a nurse.

Okay, just to get us started, tell me about your very first creative memory.

Have you ever read *My Name is Asher Lev*?

No.

It's great. In the book *My Name is Asher Lev*, the author's dad is a rabbi. His father's father was a rabbi. His grandfather was a rabbi. He's supposed to be a rabbi. But he sees.

What does he see?

As a young child, the author starts seeing perspective and shadows, and he explains that shift in this book. He becomes an artist. He explains how he was born to be an artist. He explains the process.

I saw this happen with my son Luca when he was about three. We were in the kitchen, where there was a lamp overhead, and I could see him moving his head; I explicitly remember the white table and the white milk and watching him realize that as you move, your perspective changes. When I read *My Name is Asher Lev*, I realized the same thing. I remember that. And I tell everybody, anybody who asks, I was born to do this job. I was born to be a designer. This is my dharma.

When you were young, how did you describe what it is you wanted to do in the future?

I was raised on a military base. There was no real option of being an artist. You couldn't be an artist or a writer because people just didn't do that. I came from a small town in upstate New York. I remember coming out of high school and people saying, "Well, I hear there's good money in nursing. You should go into nursing."

James Victore, R.N.

Yes! I thought it was ludicrous, but I still didn't know that I could be a designer for a living. Nevertheless, I drew constantly. I was always making up wordplays and bad puns and creating new lyrics for songs. I'd make up lyrics to Led Zeppelin songs that I didn't understand.

The only person I know in the business who thinks like this is Emily Oberman. She and I both thrive on word association. We get triggered—bzzzzzz—and off we go to find all these other associations. And that's how I work. That's what I do with my job.

Do you remember the moment you made the decision to become a designer?

Well, when I first got out of high school, I didn't get into any of my universities of choice because my grades weren't good enough.

What were you intending to study?

Engineering or physics. I became a physics major at the State University of New York at Plattsburgh. I did horribly, and I was asked not to come back for the second semester.

You were kicked out?

Yes, I was kicked out. So I went to work for my father. He had a ski shop. I also waited tables. And I slept in my car. I was crying a lot. It was like, "What the fuck?" Then my dad gave me a card from someone who came by the ski shop. He was from a design and advertising agency. This was something I'd never heard of. So I put some drawings in a folder, and I went to the guy and he was like, "Yeah, okay. We need some help." He had a tiny little advertising agency, and they made menus and fliers for dry cleaners. That's what they did. But he recognized something in me.

Through him, I got the idea to apply to art school. So I applied to RISD, the Museum of Fine Arts in Boston, the School of the Art Institute of Chicago, Pratt, SVA, and Cooper Union. The only school I didn't get into was Cooper Union. I made the decision to go to SVA primarily because I wanted to go to New York City: the city of vision, the city of light. That was where I wanted to be.

I left with 350 bucks in my pocket, and I showed up at school. But when I was there, I questioned whether or not I belonged there. I couldn't help but think that I was not like these people around me.

Why weren't you like them?

I just felt that I didn't belong. I was living in the YMCA on 34th street. My classes weren't that interesting, and I was supposed to be studying art and design in New York—and I just wasn't that interested. So I dropped out.

What did you do then?

I had one instructor in my second year, the graphic designer Paul Bacon. He gave me a D. But when I dropped out of school, I went to his office and said that I'd like to apprentice. I didn't even know what it meant, but I wanted to apprentice with him. He looked at me and put his pen down and told me that no one had ever asked him that before. Then he agreed to let me do it. I learned a huge lesson at that moment: You have got to ask. I got that apprenticeship because no one else had ever asked.

So I started hanging out in Paul's studio, looking over his shoulder. I'd get there in the morning and sweep; I didn't really have any jobs. And then I'd hang out. When a desk became available, I tried to do some "real" design. Three months after I dropped out of SVA, I had put together a portfolio with three fake book jackets. I started showing my portfolio, and I got hired right off the bat. I've been working ever since.

What do you do when you have a client who gives you negative feedback?

HOW TO THINK LIKE A GREAT GRAPHIC DESIGNER

We are professionals. We do not care about negative feedback.

There are some designers who would say, "Do it my way or bye-bye."

No. No, no, no, no. This is what we do for a living. The unspoken part of what we do is compromise. Clients don't just come to me and say, "James Victore, he's the auteur, we'll let him do what he wants." I have very little of that. And the funny thing is, when I was a young Turk and trying to push my elbows out as wide as possible, I had the opportunity. I knew a guy in town, Pierre Bernard. I knew of his reputation, so I searched him out and arranged to meet him. He is an amazing French designer from Grapus, a design collective that broke up in 1989.

He spent an afternoon with me, which was unheard of, since I was a nobody. As I was showing him my work—a greeting card I was doing at the time—I bragged that I had an amazing client who gave me complete creative freedom. He looked at my work and said, "Sometimes complete creative freedom is not a good thing." That was excellent.

I don't really want complete creative freedom. A lot of people look at my work and think I must have complete freedom, but that's not what I do. Saul Steinberg couldn't entertain the idea of working for a client. Paul Rand could. He needed a client. He needed "The Job." When I worked for *The New York Times* for a short stint, I called Saul Steinberg to do a project, and he said to me, "Let me get this correct. You want me to illustrate somebody else's idea? It seems there are two artists on this project."

Do you consider your work to be good?

I consider my work good. I enjoy doing it, which helps a lot. Unfortunately, I get a lot of feedback, constantly, from people who write me about my work. But I know when I'm "giving one from

column A, one from column B." Overall, I think
my work is pretty good, but I don't think it's great.

*What do you mean by "giving one from column A and
one from column B"?*

The rule here is there are jobs you do for "god," and
there are jobs you do for money. I try to approach
everything as a "god job"—lowercase *g*. At the beginning of a project, I ask, "What are we going to do,
and how are we going to do it? How are we going to
make a person fall in love?" And when we start getting questionable feedback about what we've done,
we have to realize it's not always possible to do the
god job. That's when I know we just have to get it
done and get paid.

*How do you know when something you've designed
is great?*

I don't. Quite frankly, I don't. Sometimes I think
something is awesome, and everyone else thinks
it's crap.

*How confident are you in your own judgment or
assessment of things?*

Less and less as time goes on. Less and less. I'm
wrong a lot more than I think. And that's why I have
other people to check me, like my wife, Laura, and
my son. As I progress and get older, I want my world
to get bigger and bigger and bigger, not smaller and
smaller and smaller. But I find that it takes constant
effort. I'm not a good judge of my work or other
people's. Especially other people's!

What do you worry about in your life?

Professionally, I don't really have any worries. Any.
I like what I do. But I am worried about what the
state of the profession will be in the future. I'm
worried about the state of the world. My concern
now is to make a little bit of money. And for the first
time in my life, I feel guilty about it.

Why do you feel guilty about it?

In regard to the state of the world. Laura is currently reading Charles Dickens' *A Christmas Carol*. In the book, when [Jacob] Marley's Ghost comes to Scrooge, Scrooge says, "But you were always a good man of business, Jacob!" "Business!" cries the Ghost. "Mankind was my business. The common welfare was my business. Charity, mercy, forbearance, and benevolence were all my business. The dealings of my trade were but a drop of water in the comprehensive ocean of my business." This is what I worry about.

I like what I do, and I seem to have a reputation for altruism and telling the truth; but at the same time, all that work I do for free. Or I pay for it with my own money. And now I'm worried about making a living for my family. And this bothers me because I don't know how to do both. And I want a hot rod!

I was just reading about Nan Kempner and her desire to have nice things.

I remember Tibor used to say, "I want to take taxis."

You mentioned that you were worried about the future of the design business?

The business as *I* know it. The Internet is changing things in the same way that the invention of ink on paper did. And there is this wonderful, funny question that people like to ask all the time: "Are posters dead?" It's like asking Twyla Tharp, "Is dance dead?" People try to reorganize and rename things and change them and qualify and quantify them. I just want the spirit of design to remain.

I feel now the way Tibor did: People have not fucked with the printed page as much as we still can.

I want those opportunities. But I think those opportunities get fewer and fewer.

And there's too many of us. But there aren't enough crackpots and artists in the business— they're all MBAs.

Who do you think right now is a crackpot and an artist in the business?

Any of the designers who are 50 and older. They were around before computers. They were working with their hands. Most younger designers don't do that.

You work both on the computer and with your hands. Are you equally comfortable with both mediums?

No, I'm dreadful on the computer.

How do you know when a project is done, aside from a deadline?

I asked Pat Duniho that question, because he could draw like a motherfucker. It was beautiful. I asked him how he knew when he was done. And he said, "Well, you have a big piece of paper like this. And you start in the middle and you fill it out and when you reach the edge of the paper, you're done."

Knowing when you're done is essential. That is where most people falter. I think we're so in love with the fact that we can do this thing called design, and when we get the opportunity, we just want to do it so much! Especially when you get pro bono opportunities. The not-for-profit stuff is the shit because it's our opportunity to go off and get really creative.

But knowing when you're done is hard.

The thing that's great about this profession— and doing it well—is that it's like medicine. Doctors can see a patient get sick and die, or they can help them get better. We can do that with our business, to a certain extent. You know you've done a good job when you can see positive change. That is the most awesome feeling in the world.

You mentioned that a lot of people write and tell you how much they've been impacted by your work. What do you think touches people so profoundly?

> I don't know. I got a message from someone this morning telling me he liked the way I told the truth.

How do you think you tell the truth?

> I think I either get the opportunity or I go looking for it. Sometimes I have to go digging for it. There are surface—veneer—solutions to design problems, and that's appropriate if you're talking bullshit. But to get to the truth, you have to push everything aside. Everything—and then get down to that one perfect little gem.

How do you know when it's a gem?

> I talk to my students about that all the time.

It's about whittling. It's about taking something and whittling and whittling and getting it sharp and perfect. Then you've got something.

Do those things come instantly after all the whittling away?

> No, a lot of the time it comes as a surprise. It's hard work. It's the time when I'm sitting at the table, and I've been working on something for hours and hours and I come up with something and I make myself laugh. That's what I do. And I'll ask Laura to come and look at it. And she'll either say, "That's funny," or she says it's funny *and* she laughs. When she does that, I know I'm good as gold.

Is it about being funny, or is it about making a connection to something that might not have been done before?

> Yes, it's definitely finding another way to say something. It's about realizing that you have kept

something in your mental files forever, and now you're going to take it out.

Do you think it takes a special type of mentality for a viewer to love your work?

I don't think so. I think it takes a special type of mentality to not get uptight about my work, a special type of mentality to have a sense of humor about it.

I've read that people believe that in your work, you're able to communicate what other people are afraid to say. Is that something that you've consciously worked on being able to do?

No. I'm just inappropriate. That's who I am. I have a foul mouth, and I like off-color jokes—but I'm not a boorish, Shakespeare's Richard kind of character.

How would you describe yourself?

I like to think that I'm strong and quick to judge. But at the same time—similar to when I am talking to my son—I am extremely stern, but full of love.

How content are you?

Not. Never have been, never will be. I don't think it's possible—unfortunately. It's something I want.

Do you think that's what fuels you?

Yes. I wake up in the morning knowing I've got to start at 5 or 5:30. I've got to get downstairs, I've got to get working. I've got to sit on the couch and start studying, or I've got to go run. And I don't do that because it's naturally in me. I do it because I have to force myself to do it, because I know that if I don't, I'll be a wreck.

What do you mean by that?

I push myself really hard. I live by lists. I have today's lists, I have my short-term list, I have my

long-term list. It makes me immeasurably happy
when I cross something off one of my lists.

Are you a control freak?

I have to be. I think we all have to be in this business. I try not to show it in my work, but I think
I am. Definitely.

If you didn't push yourself so hard, what would happen?

I don't know. I don't know. Probably nothing. I just
like doing it. It makes me feel like I'm progressing.
It makes me feel like I'm getting things done. If I
could include "brush teeth," it would be on the list.
But it's not. Sometimes I recognize that I'm not
doing something on the list because of fear; and
I see that in myself and I'm like, "Nope. Do it. Do it.
Do it."

Do you consider yourself to be afraid of a lot of things?

Yes. I'm afraid of everything. I am. But I do them
anyway. This is my dharma. This is what I was
meant to do. I just want to do a good job.

John Maeda

*The graphic designer John Maeda is best known as a
multimedia artist, teacher, and theorist. A longtime
professor at the storied MIT Media Lab, Maeda has
helped to invent the language, grammar, and technology of digital interactivity. His work has been shown
in single-person exhibitions at such prestigious institutions as France's Fondation Cartier. As part of his
professorial responsibilities, he has mentored a legion
of students who themselves have gone on to become
significant figures in the field.*

*Maeda's work and research now focuses in
part on simplifying complex systems, and he is on
a quest to whittle down the sometimes bewildering
intricacies of software and interactivity in an effort
to "humanize" technology. Reducing things to a minimum is perhaps a natural reaction to the seeming
complexity of his own life. In addition to his duties
at MIT, Maeda is father of five daughters, writes
two blogs, and recently finished an MBA. It would
seem that Maeda has little time for anything else,
and yet he continues to create art, write books,
consult with businesses, and advise organizations
such as the Smithsonian's Cooper-Hewitt National
Design Museum.*

*In our discussion, John talks about his favorite
typeface, how it's more interesting having a friend
than a project, Christina Aguilera's pop songs, and
what Paul Rand taught him about making lots
of money.*

What was your first creative memory?

My first creative memory was working with cardboard.

In what way?

When I was growing up, my family didn't have a lot of money. We lived near a tofu factory, and we had a lot of cardboard boxes there. I used to play with them and make architecture and weapons.

When you were very little, what did you want to be when you grew up?

I wanted to be a dentist.

A dentist! Why is that?

Because one of our family friends was a dentist, and my father thought it would be a good career for me. We also knew an aerospace engineer who lived in Seattle, where Boeing is located. These were my influences.

So when did you first realize you wanted to be a designer?

When I was a sophomore at MIT. People told me I had a knack for visual presentations and making icons. And they told me about this field called "design." I was like, hmmmm, what is that? So I went out and bought a book on advertising. It was one of those compendiums, those annuals.

Do you remember who wrote it?

It was one of these strange, unreadable Japanese titles that I saw in a store in Dallas, Texas. But I also found a book by Herb Lubalin, and I was like, wow, this is really clever! He's messing with the type! That's how I got curious about the discipline.

In applying to MIT, what did you aspire to be?

Really, I had no idea. When you see kids now in high

school, they are so centered, and they understand the world so well. I had no idea what I wanted to do. I just knew that I wanted to do something better than making tofu.

If someone didn't know anything about you, and they asked what you do for a living, how would you describe yourself? Would you describe yourself as a graphic designer?

I think I've always grappled with that. Basically, I say I'm a professor.

You typically work with a lot of other people. Do you also work alone?

I actually work alone in general. That's why I'm a bad role model as a designer.

Why is that?

Because I make everything by myself. I design everything by myself. I shoot all the photographs, I do all the cropping. I manipulate all the elements in Quark, Photoshop, etc. I don't know how to have assistance because when I was starting out, I thought all these people did these things by themselves. When you meet famous designers, you realize that they have giant teams that pump out the work from the basic art-directed form they are given by the famous designer. I never knew about this, so I always art-direct myself.

Do you ever work by hand, or do you primarily work with technology?

Oh, both, definitely. I often sketch on paper—I feel that it's most natural. The computer always comes at the very end.

Do you find that you have any process for initiating your design work?

I used to be very heavily airplane-bound.

Airplane-bound?

I was flying on airplanes a lot. On an airplane, you're trapped. Well, this was before on-demand video.

On-demand video has changed your design process?

Well, now I'm tempted to watch something, but before, I would sit there and draw because there was nothing else to do. It was crammed. I'm not a big guy, so even on small, confined airplanes, I could get seats where I was able to draw and create and think on paper. Now, I'm just listening to Paul Rand's advice.

Which is?

Well, back when I was a student, I visited his studio for one day. Coincidentally, his assistant hadn't arrived that day, so he had me work for him for that one day. It was just the two of us, and all of a sudden, he got very quiet. Then he said, "I've got something really important to tell you." Now remember, I had just met him. And I asked, "What, what do you have to tell me?" And he said, "Make lots of money."

That's what he told you?

Yes. He must have seen my look of horror, because he added, "Oh no, don't get me wrong. The things you really love to do in life will make you absolutely no money. And the things that do make the money for you are different. There is stuff that is work. So you do the work to do what you love to do." It made sense. Whenever you start something without constraints, it's always better. And when it becomes a job, it changes. It's a simple philosophy, I think. But I always go back to that saying. Having some money gives you the freedom to explore what you want to do. But earning money is often not freedom.

When you're working on a project, how do you know if something you're doing is good?

When the time runs out. I think it's as simple as that. I think all people who work—all creative people who make things for other people (this can be designers or cooks or anyone)—are highly dependent on time. You ask the client when they need it by, and you scale your time accordingly.

Well, that would mean that you think that when the work is finished, it's good.

When I say it's good, it's good enough.

How do you know if you have done something really brilliant?

I never feel that way.

Never?

I've never been happy with the work I've done. I wish I were. I've seen people who were happy. I think I'm always wondering what else the end result could have been.

Do you look back on your work and wish you had done a lot of things differently?

I do a lot of different types of things, and I try not to focus on looking back because it makes me depressed.

Do you find that you can assess your own work or are you highly dependent on other people's opinions?

I think that anybody can assess their own work. I also think that others can assess it, and that opinion will be varied in many ways. My wife is my most ardent critic. I'm lucky to have such a critical person in my life. She'll tell me, "Hey, you did that already." So she's always been there for me in that way. But in the grand scheme of things, once a project is done, the next job happens. The client is busy. You're busy. Maybe if you're lucky, you've made a deep relationship. That's the most important thing. I'm finding right now, as you age, work doesn't matter as much. Friends matter much more. It's more interesting having a friend than having a project.

How confident are you in your own judgment?

Not at all. And that's another quality I admired about Paul Rand. When I was working on *From Lascaux to Brooklyn*, there was something that I found that looked odd. I thought the rag didn't look right. I showed it to Paul, and I told him I could fix it. And he said, "What do you mean?" I asked, "Isn't it kind of off?" And he changed his posture, and he said, "If I say it's right, it's right." And I thought that was amazing.

Now, when I teach students, I always remember this. It makes it hard to have critiques, though. One of my students was educated at Yale in graphic design. He told me, "John, you're never critical with your students." And I am not. Maybe this is good. Maybe it's bad. But I personally don't believe there's good and bad. Maybe if I make it to the age of 82 like Paul Rand, I might have the right to say "what is good" and what isn't.

I think the role of a teacher is to imbue confidence in students, to encourage them to be curious and to take chances. The one teacher that influenced me more than any other was the first teacher who made me feel like I could be smart.

Were there other key influences?

I cannot forget when I was learning typography, one of my teachers sat me down in his office and lectured me and told me how I would never amount to anything at all in my life. In some ways, I appreciate that this happened because it made me evaluate what I was doing, and at the same time, it made me realize I would never want to do this to someone else.

Do you feel that there is any objectivity in
assessing design?

> I think the one point of objectivity, as Paul Rand
> always said, is relevance. Not just relevance to
> message, but relevance to cultural timing. Often-
> times that means it's off time.

Do you consider yourself to be more of an intuitive
designer or more intellectual?

> I was so influenced by the grid early on. It was use-
> ful. But then I began to embrace the "what the hell"
> kind of viewpoint.

Do you do a lot of research before you start a project?

> I think I should. I think, though, I am always
> researching the world in general. I always have
> a camera. I'm always curious about things. Even
> walking across the street, there is so much to
> learn by what you see. In the puddles, in the sky,
> in the flowers, in the trash. Every person's world
> is a museum.

How many books do you read a year?

> An increasing number. Which I'm not sure is a good
> thing or a bad thing.

Why?

> I used to read very little. I used to skim more. And
> now I find myself reading more, and yes, I do think
> I appreciate more, but I also think that by reading
> more, I'm doing less.

Do you feel like you are very involved with or
influenced by contemporary culture?

> Yes, definitely. But that's because I have kids. And
> the kids are always telling me about "the latest,"
> so I know all the latest pop songs…

Anything that you would consider to be a favorite?

> Well, even at my age, I'm a Christina Aguilera fan. I

love her song "Fighter." It's semi-autobiographical, but it's all about how when she was young, she was made fun of at the playground for being different. In the song, she basically thanks everyone for making her a fighter. I think it's an empowering message: Especially for girls, which is very, very important.

Would you consider yourself to be a control freak?
I'm trying to be much less so.

So that means yes, but no.
Yes, but no. Particularly around people. These days, I'm more involved with managerial issues. I see that the same sensitivity you can have with an A4 sheet does not apply to people, because people are not on a grid. People don't behave perfectly.

How do you think most people would describe you?
I don't know. I'm not sure. I try not to care, I guess. I think when you start to care, you fixate and you want to change too many things. A doctor friend of mine told me never to get your body scanned. They have these machines for people, and they can scan your body and tell you what's wrong with you. She's a doctor and she warned me to never do this. Because you'll always find something wrong. And once you find something wrong, you're going to go after it. And oftentimes, going after it can damage you even more. But it's hard not caring what people think about you. **That's why I keep changing what I'm doing—to avoid criticism.**

Do you ever worry?
Worry? Yes, I worry. I worry. I worry about my health, always. I worry about my family. I don't worry about too many other things, though. I don't worry about work or how a project turns out.

Why not?

No matter how much you worry, it's not going to change the outcome. Also, work is very cyclical. Sometimes you're up, and sometimes you're down.

Would you say that you're confident about your work?

Me? No, I think if I were, I would stop doing what I'm doing and live off my laurels.

Really?

Yes. But I'm not confident, so I keep trying something new.

What's your most favorite thing to do?

Um, sleep.

What's your favorite typeface?

Favorite typeface, now that's an important question. I don't know anymore. I think the correct choice is something classic that no one really cares about, like Helvetica. I think I like my own handwriting the best. Right now.

That's interesting. Any least favorite typeface?

The typeface doesn't really matter, as long as the text is good. I love text. Just text itself, instead of the type. I think designers fail to remember that.

What do you mean?

They fail to remember that text is more powerful than graphics.

Why do you think that's so?

Because text is the ultimate form of distraction. Text is going through all these weird layers of our brain to try to become understood. I find that interesting. Very, very interesting.

Paul Sahre

One of the most telling details about Paul Sahre is the acronym of his studio's name, Office of Paul Sahre, which is featured in a neon sign overlooking a section of New York's Sixth Avenue. Ironic, humorous, and clever, the O.O.P.S. abbreviation embodies the spirit and witty sensibility of this incredibly talented graphic designer.

Paul does a wide range of both commercial and personal projects. His office is an eclectic workspace that incorporates elements of a design studio, a foosball arena, and a silk-screen shop. Like this space, Sahre's design sensibility can't be pinned down to one category. Silk-screening may be one dimension of his aesthetic panoply, but Sahre is equally expressive with illustration and photography, as evidenced in projects such as a book cover for Rick Moody, visual commentaries for The New York Times' Op-Ed *page, and his sublime illustrations for the jazz label Smalls Records.*

Paul and I met in his studio, located above a Dunkin' Donuts. We sat and drank coffee while Paul talked about his early wish to be a professional baseball player, his desire to draw like Charles Schulz, and the insight he gained from watching designer Alexander Gelman perch a hot cup of coffee at the edge of a desk. After our interview, he taught me how to play foosball under the neon halo of the O.O.P.S. sign in his third-floor window.

*What was your first creative memory, or when do you
first remember being creative in your life?*

> I always drew. From my earliest memories, I was
> the artist in the family, constantly drawing.

Do you remember your first drawing?

> I made a Christmas ornament, shaped as the head
> of a baseball player, that is still on my mom's tree.

When did you decide to go into graphic design?

> I didn't. I thought it was commercial art—my
> father had to go out and encourage his lazy son to
> do something with his future. So he went out and
> bought a book about design and told me I should
> go to an accredited college. It's funny; my dad, the
> aerospace engineer, was the one who pushed me
> into graphic design.

What was it about commercial art that interested you?

> When I was a kid, I wanted to be a cartoonist. I
> wanted to be Charles Schulz, so I had invented
> this lame character called Wentworth, a baboon.
> I have a couple of comics still left over to this day.
> I thought I was going to make my fortune being like
> Charles Schulz. I remember reading that he owned
> an ice rink. That was so cool. I was like, "I want an
> ice rink."

What was it about Peanuts *or Charles Schulz that
intrigued you? Do you have a sense of what it was that
you admired?*

> I grew up in a very blue-collar town in upstate New
> York. There wasn't a lot of creativity happening
> there in general. I think the thing about comics is
> that they are everywhere. They're in all the daily
> papers and in books. They're a part of popular
> culture. Becoming a cartoonist is an ambition that's
> more of a mass aspiration; it wasn't deciding I was
> going to do something because I love to do it. It was
> more like, "Oh look. Everyone will love me if I do

this funny thing!" The reason I drew wasn't necessarily because I love drawing.

So what happened when you were in college?

I'm not really sure. But I think my going to school
was less a choice and more of a "this is what I have
to do." I played a lot of sports as a kid, and my first
choice for a career would have been to become a
professional baseball player. That is probably
where my passion was as a kid. When I realized
that this wasn't going to happen, I decided to see
if I could transform this other thing I do well into
a career.

And you chose Kent State?

I chose Kent State for a couple of different reasons.
One, because of my Wonder Bread kind of upbring-
ing. It was very *Brady Bunch*, with more arguments.
It was a fucked-up version of *The Brady Bunch*. I
just wanted to get the fuck out of there. I wanted to
go far enough away so I could at least get away and
be away, but I still felt a pull to be fairly close. Ohio
was about a ten-hour drive. When I told my parents
I wanted to go to Kent State, their response was,
"Kent State? Isn't that where they shoot students?"
And to be honest, that was part of the draw. It felt
like a radical place to go to school.

Did Kent State have a good design department?

The Kent State design program was run by Charles
Walker; he had attended the University of Cincin-
nati program as a graduate student. Kent State was
a Swiss-based international school, a great program
that was very rigorous. I couldn't tell you the actual
numbers, but I know there were more than 100
people who started in my freshman class, and eight
of us staggered across the finish line as seniors.

Charles was crazy. He was very militant about
design. He felt very strongly that it was irrespon-
sible to send people through a revolving door and

then release them into the profession without being prepared.

I had absolutely no idea what I was getting into. And I'll tell you what: The thing that got me through initially was my drawing skills.

Looking back on it now, is there anything else you might have wanted to be?

No. I love what I'm doing now. I believe that I'm doing the very thing I was meant to do. I know it sounds cheesy. But I think it worked out perfectly, even though I didn't have much of a plan. At some point during college, I got it. I found I could not satisfy my thirst for information. I pulled all-nighters; I found myself reading all the time, bugging professors, and getting in people's faces. I became a whirlwind of absorbing knowledge. That's when something new started happening. And I came out from college a different person than when I went in.

Can you identify what it is about design that you love so much?

It's complex. Part of it is this: You have an idea, and you can make that idea real. I think it's much more complex than that, but I think you can make your ideas happen without a filter. You wouldn't think that would describe graphic design necessarily. Usually if you're doing graphic design, it's "applied art," so there's normally a client involved or some external concern that you're addressing.

I think what I love most is that I can use graphic design as a vehicle for expressing myself. This represents for me a dichotomy inherent in graphic design, though it doesn't really jibe with what graphic design actually is. It's a very selfish way of approaching it. Graphic design is, at its core, more of an altruistic activity. You're helping someone else express a message in an appropriate way, or in a way that's memorable. But I strongly believe that design is a dichotomy.

Design is supposed to be about something else, and not about you; but I think the only way it's actually any good—and to get people to care about it—is if it's also about you at the same time.

Really? You believe that it needs to be about you and the client at the same time?

I think it does. Designers have to feel it's theirs. They have to have a sense of authorship and owner-ship. And I think designers who aren't selfish do really awful work.

Really? Why is that?

I think that there needs to be a motivation at the core of the work. There needs to be a motivation for the designer to go beyond the point where most people would stop. I think we do this because we are going to somehow benefit from it. There are some designers who do it because they're benefiting from money. Or they're benefiting by finding a forum where they can express themselves. But I actually think that the dichotomy is what makes it interesting. It makes it harder.

If you're doing something for a client, but it has to be something that you bring yourself into, and it's also about something that you need to do—those two motivations do not meet. They're total opposites. Like oil and vinegar; you've got to mix it up, and maybe that's the reason why most designers have a very difficult time keeping clients for a long period of time.

Why is that?

If it's mine *and* yours, then wait a minute: It's mine. Maybe there's something to that. I think that's what makes it difficult, and in many ways, it is impossible to satisfy both sides. There is always a tension there. But I think the tension is what makes it interesting.

*Would you say that this "selfishness" is apparent in the
work? Or is it something perhaps only you could identify?*

> I hope it's something only I can identify. Because it's
> filtered through this way of thinking that's altruistic
> on the face of it.

**But there are many
times when I get my greatest joy from being totally
invisible in terms of the viewer. They don't know someone designed what they are looking at! Nevertheless, it's
still something that I needed to express a certain way.**

*If you don't feel that you're emotionally involved with
the work you're doing, do you feel it's possible to do
something that is creatively successful?*

> Yes. But I think "successful" and "someone who's
> really caring about it and changing someone's mind
> about it" are two different things.

*How do you know when something you've designed is
successful?*

> It's a little thing, a little spark that makes something
> memorable or beautiful or unforgettable. It's very
> hard to describe and people have very different
> ways of describing it. [Alexander] Gelman once
> came into my class at the School of Visual Arts,
> and he was trying to describe this very thing in my
> two-dimensional design theory class. He said that
> the thing we're shooting for is to create a dynamic
> design. He always comes to the class with a hot
> cup of coffee—because he knows he's going to do
> this—and says, "What you want your work to do is,
> you want your work to do this—..."
>
> And he spends five minutes trying to get the
> hot cup of coffee on the edge of the desk so it's just
> right at that very point where it might go. No one
> can take their eyes off of it. And that's what I try
> to do with my work.

How do you know when you've achieved that?

I don't know. I don't know if I can answer that. That gets to a larger question about what your process is and how you arrive at things. But I'm a firm believer in logic and creative thinking and being able to think your way through the process and arrive at a solution that makes sense and is going to be effective. It's applied design. I think that's crucial; I don't think you can be a graphic designer without it. But I also don't believe that you can be a graphic designer without the intuitive side, the side that just goes, "Aha!" You can't describe it. If you try, you're probably going to fail. And I think you have to operate with both of those things working—if not simultaneously, at least one letting the other play for a while.

How confident are you in your own judgment?

I feel as time has progressed, I've gotten much more confident about making a decision and just living with it. An architect would probably laugh at this; but as a graphic designer, you're responsible for large quantities being produced from this thing that you made, and there's a certain pressure there. It's like, "Oh shit! There it goes out into the world." You can't fix it after it's printed. And I remember feeling a really strong sense of pressure with that when I was younger. I think it's natural that you would.

Several years ago, I saw a lecture by the photographer Jayme Odgers. And he was describing the zone that he likes to get into when he's making something. That's the time wherein you don't even notice that time's passing. Maybe you've got a headache or your knuckles are bleeding. But you're so focused on what you're doing that nothing else matters. Odgers said that from the time he gets up in the morning to the time he goes to bed at night, he strives to be in the zone as much as he possibly can. I totally understand what he's talking about.

I don't know if it necessarily makes for an ordered life. If you live like this, there are probably a lot of things that go by the wayside.

For example?

Well, if you were in that zone, you are not calling your family, you are probably eating fast food. I missed my nephew's birthday recently. I was on the phone with him apologizing. He's eleven, and missing his birthday was not cool.

Whenever I talk about things humans get obsessed with, I realize it's all the same. Whether it's surfing, or graphic design, or ballroom dancing, or Scrabble. It's all the same shit, you know? It's all the same core need, but I don't know how to describe it any better. Perhaps it's because we think we're all going to die and nobody's going to know we were here. But there's something in doing something you love that's very similar, no matter what it is. Perhaps it's the obsession—the wonderful obsession.

Graphic design is my obsession. Deep in my love of graphic design is proof that I can leave for my children. They'll know.

How would you like to be remembered?

I guess I'd like to be remembered as somebody who cared about and believed in what he did. I'd like to think that I'm leaving a trail behind me. I know that there are certain designers who are no longer with us, and you can almost crawl inside their heads and spend some time with them, even though they're not around anymore. I'm thinking about people like John Heartfield. You look at some of the work he was doing, and even the way he would credit his work: I feel an incredible connection with him, even though I never met the man.

I feel the same way about Jack Kirby. I can see some of the things that he was doing, and see where he was struggling, or where he had to rush, or where he had to make a concession that he didn't want to. I can even see a situation where he had too much control and fucked something up. I can totally see that.

I think leaving good work behind is the most important thing for me. I'm in my early forties now, so I don't think about this very much. But I would be very upset if all my work just vanished. It's certainly not the only reason to do things, but it's definitely a part of it. You make this thing and can put it over there. And then you can go and make some more! And these things are going to be around in certain forms—even the stuff that you're embarrassed by—long after you're gone. I never want to take the easy way.

Chip Kidd

*My fascination with books began as soon as I learned
to read, and the Golden Books imprint was my
favorite. By third grade, I became acquainted with
the Scholastic Book Club, and I used my allowance
to order as many titles as I could afford. When the
boxes arrived, I'd sit for a minute or two and imagine
what was inside, what the books would be like, and,
of course, how they would look. Always how they
would look.*

*There is no one who has had more impact on
the design of contemporary books than Chip Kidd.
His book jackets for Alfred A. Knopf have helped
spark a revolution in the art of American book packaging. He has created over 1,500 covers, including
works for Bret Easton Ellis, David Sedaris, Michael
Crichton, Cormac McCarthy, and many others.*

*Equally capable as a designer, writer, and edi-
tor, Kidd has authored books—such as the critically
acclaimed* Batman Collected—*in which he shares his
enthusiasms for graphic design and popular culture.
Kidd has also been generous in revealing his successes,
failures, and learning process to an audience of admirers, as he demonstrates in the remarkable monograph*
Chip Kidd: Book One: Work: 1986–2006 *and in his
semi-autobiographical novel* The Cheese Monkeys,
*the story of a design student's coming-of-age. He was
similarly forthcoming in our conversation.*

What was your first creative memory?

Making poopies. And some critics have pointed out that I've never really advanced beyond that.

As a child, what did you want to be when you grew up?

I have gone on public record as saying that I wanted more than anything to be Chris Partridge in *The Partridge Family* on TV. For your readers under 40, I should explain that he was an eight-year-old professional rock drummer. No further explanation necessary.

When did you realize that you wanted to be a graphic designer?

I remember in sixth grade or so, we had an assignment in art class to make a record album cover for one of our favorite songs. I picked "Fly, Robin, Fly" by the Silver Convention, and drew a 45 rpm record with wings sprouting out of its sides, soaring through a watercolor sky flecked with cotton-ball clouds. It was so, so beautiful. And meaningful.

Did you ever have serious aspirations to pursue any other type of career?

I played the drums from third grade through college (hence Chris Partridge) and ultimately had to decide between pursuing a career in music and a career in graphic design.

Why didn't you pursue drumming?

If there's anything harder to become successful at than music, it is certainly not graphic design.

What did you study in college?

I did the "legit" thing and majored in graphic design as an undergrad at Penn State. That worked well for me, and I saw no sense in graduate school at all. I should also add that I have been ever grateful that I went to a university that required a full BA's worth of classes, instead of an art school. A graphic designer has to function in the world. We need to know more than just typefaces and Pantone colors—indeed, that's the least of it. I learned just as much about design by studying psychology, philosophy, English lit, geology, art history and, yes, ballroom dancing.

How would you define the term "graphic design"?

Entire books have been written about that, so I will keep my answer brief, boring, and technical. If design is, simply, purposeful planning, then graphic design is such involving the use of a visual medium—pictures, words, or a combination of the two. Yawn.

Do you typically work alone or with other people?

Both, actually. By that, I mean I usually design everything by myself, but I'm also on staff at Knopf, which means there are ten-plus designers just steps down the hall. And they are ten-plus *great* designers. We bounce stuff off of each other all the time, and it's extremely helpful and encouraging. It's the best of both worlds, actually. I wouldn't be able to stay at home or in a studio alone and work in a complete vacuum. I know that works great for some people, but I need to be around others who are also making things. It's very inspiring.

Do you work primarily by hand or with a computer?

Almost completely by computer, especially if I'm writing. But even back in school, well before the Mac came along, I was not big on sketching—I just don't have the "sketch" impulse. I always tried to show work in as completed a form as possible, even at the rough stage. And of course the computer makes that a zillion times easier. That said, I do think that any worthy graphic design program should first teach kids to solve problems using their heads and their hands and leave the computer out of it.

Do you find that you have a process for initiating your design work?

The process starts with getting the assignment, which is usually to read a manuscript of a book I have to do the cover for. Then it can go any number of ways. If I don't have a clear sense of what I should do, I'm instantly filled with dread, which hangs over me like a thin, stinky fog until I either figure out a way to solve the problem or throw in the towel. I will say, though, that those "eureka" moments— when it all comes together in your head and you realize the perfect thing to do and you just know it is right, whether the client will like it or not—those are the closest moments to sex in graphic design.

Are you ever given research by your clients you must consider for a project?

Sometimes the authors do the research for you, and every now and then, they pleasantly surprise you. Both John Updike and Orhan Pamuk presented me with the art to use for their most recent covers— *Terrorist* and *Istanbul*, respectively—and in both cases, they were terrific. Sure made my job easier.

How do you feel when a project is completed?

If it comes out well, relieved. If not, I'm at least glad it's out of my life. Regardless, I'm usually on to the next thing long before the last thing is produced.

When do you know a project is finished?

When I see it remaindered at Barnes & Noble.

How do you know when something you've created is good?

When after ten years, I can look at it and not wince, that's a good sign. Fifteen years, even better. Twenty and up—yay!

How confident are you in your own judgment?

It is all too easy to get so close to something you're working on that you lose all perspective on it and you cannot tell. In such cases, if I have the luxury of time, I'll put whatever it is away and come back to it later. Otherwise, I'd say my intuition has done me in pretty good stead.

How important to your work is writing?

In my case, extremely important, because I'm also a novelist. That sounds really pretentious, sorry. My great failing is that I've gotten so used to writing in Quark, in a text typeface, that I can't really write much of anything unless I use my laptop. I would not recommend this method to others.

I'm often asked for advice on how to become a better graphic designer, and this is my response: "Two things—learn how to do crossword puzzles, and learn how to write."

The former teaches you to think about language in a whole new way, and the latter forces you to use it. These are invaluable skills for any creative person.

Do you feel you are an intuitive designer or are you more intellectual in your approach?

I don't see a difference in the two. Unless by "intellectual" you mean a design solution that requires reams of explanation in order to understand it, in which case I'd say it's a total failure.

Do you sketch a lot?

No. I doodle a lot. And in my case that's not the same thing. Regarding jobs, occasionally I find myself having to scrawl the odd idea onto a soggy bar napkin, just to get the most rudimentary point across. But I avoid that sort of thing as much as possible.

Are you wary of people who can't draw?

Certainly not. Good draughtsmanship is a very, very difficult thing to achieve and usually requires years of dedication and hard work. What I *am* wary of, regarding this subject, is drawing that is deemed to be worthy of admiration but just leaves me scratching my head.

Do you keep a journal?

Alas, no. I just don't have the sketchbook/journal/diary gene, and I regret it terribly. I think I have a subconscious—or maybe not so subconscious—belief that the time I'd spend working on a journal could be better served by actually doing work. However, most creative people I know (especially cartoonists) do keep a journal; they find it therapeutic, and I have the greatest admiration for them. I had students at the School of Visual Arts whose personal sketchbooks were far more interesting than anything they did in the class.

Do you keep a book or files for inspiration?

Well, I do keep a scrapbook of sorts, in which I keep clippings of pullquotes from newspapers and magazines. They form a strange sort of reportorial haiku. I've been doing this for over seven years and am toying with the idea of publishing the collection. We'll see.

Do you feel that your education has fundamentally influenced your design ability?

Without my education at Penn State—from Lanny Sommese, Bill Kinser, and others—I wouldn't have gotten anywhere. Conversely, the two best examples of self-taught designers I know are David Carson and Chris Ware. They are proof that it's possible, but extremely rare, and I heartily recommend a formal design education, especially including a thorough study of the history of graphic design.

Who is your favorite graphic designer?

Non-living, I'd have to say it's a four-way tie between El Lissitzky, Alexander Rodchenko, Piet

Zwart, and Alvin Lustig. But, God, there are so many others. Living, I'd say Peter Saville, if you can call that living (sorry, Peter).

Who has influenced you most in your career as a graphic designer?

It's corny to say it, but it's the books themselves I have to design covers for that influence me the most. How could they not?

Typically, how many books do you read a year?

I'd say 30 to 40, which is a lot for me because I'm a very slow reader.

Do you read newspapers?

The New York Times, and, yes, *The New York Post*. Hey, there is no order without chaos. Often the *Times* is too discrete about a particular story, and the *Post* just goes for the jugular, which can be very refreshing. But its politics are abhorrent.

Where do you see yourself in five years? What are you doing?

The nice thing is that I can honestly say that if in five years I'm still doing what I'm doing now, that wouldn't be bad at all. However, I have a few ideas about branching out in some new directions creatively and will be pursuing them. Whether the results get past the stage of "personal projects," well, we'll see.

Do you have recurring dreams or nightmares?

It's little wonder that psychiatrists are paid to listen to other people's dreams. I mean, is there anything more boring? Although, last night I had the Ruth Gordon nude-hazing dream again, and this time she was swinging the headless goat higher than she ever had before. Does that mean I hate my mother? Hold me.

Are you afraid of anything?

Oh my God, how much time do you have? I live in almost constant terror. Here's a tiny portion of the list: cancer, vaginas, giant cockroaches, Kathy Lee Gifford's latest Christmas album, burning to death, tornados, gristle, children, choking on a small toy, the pope's unwanted advances, matted clogs of hair, root rot, Deborah Sussman's eyelash extensions, Republicans, and Sucralose. And the idea that Pat Robertson is not yet dead.

What makes you laugh?

This blind man walks into an expensive antique china shop on Madison Avenue with his huge German shepherd seeing-eye dog. No sooner does the shop clerk ask, "May I help you, sir?" than the man grips the dog's handle with both hands, braces himself, and with a great heave hauls the massive beast off the ground in a single yank, and spins him around and around. The clerk cowers in fear. Having worked up tremendous momentum, the man finally lets the dog go and sends the terrified animal flying across the room, landing with a thunderous crash against an entire wall of priceless Ming vases, which explode into a million pieces. Then the man says, "No thanks, I'm just looking."

How content are you with your life?

It's not that simple.

I'd say that there are aspects of my life I'm very content with, and yet I'll always be consumed with an intense yearning, and I think that's necessary—total contentment can be a dangerous thing for a creative person.

Do you regret anything?

I regret not making the effort to meet Charles Schulz in his lifetime. I tried to make up for it by putting together a book that pays proper homage to his work. I think I was only partially successful.

What do you think of the state of contemporary graphic design?

I think of it as little as possible.

What do you think of Ken Garland's 1964 First Things First manifesto?

However well-intended, I think it was pretentious nonsense. But I suppose I'm lucky enough to be in a position to say so. As the rabbi said, "Our task is to get on with the work." The least effective way to do that is talking about what "we think" about it.

What about First Things First 2000?

Ditto. I've always considered myself to be very responsible about what I work on and how I work on it. That's just common sense, and I don't need a parcel of pseudo-intellectual claptrap (I'm referring to the manifesto itself, not necessarily the people who signed it) to tell me what to do.

What's your response to Milton Glaser's "12 Steps on the Road to Hell"? What number have you crossed?

I think it's amusing and certainly to be considered. But the only one that applies to me is number four: "Have you ever designed the jacket for a book that contains sexual content you find personally repellent?" For someone in the publishing business, this question is laughable in its oversimplification. There are entire libraries full of books with repellent sexual content that have won the Pulitzer Prize, the National Book Award, the Nobel, etc. *Lolita* is one long ode to pedophilia—which I find personally repellent, duh—and one of the best books I've ever read. I've designed a cover for a Brazilian edition of it and would do so again in a heartbeat. I think a better question would regard a given book's intent.

For example, I would flat-out refuse to design a book cover for Ann Coulter or Bill O'Reilly.

Do you think graphic designers have any obligation to create design to inspire social change?

Yes, if that is your job. But it's not implicit in the profession as a whole, and sometimes the social change that is "inspired" is not such a great thing.

Fascism in Italy did very well by some extremely beautiful art deco graphics and architecture. I think what you mean to say is "inspire positive social change." I try to do that whenever I can, say for a *New York Times* Op-Ed piece or a political poster. But in my regular line of work, it's the books themselves that have the far greater potential to affect and benefit the culture, not the jackets. And that's just fine.

What do you love most about being a graphic designer?

Making things, and then having the things you make. In that sense, I'm a total materialist and not at all ashamed of it. I have been extremely privileged for the last 20 years to put together my own personal library of sorts, assembling great books that I've been lucky enough to design the covers for.

Is there anything you dislike about being a graphic designer?

There are so many other things I want to do, and time is running out. But I truly love what I do and am thankful I'm able to keep doing it. I should also add that I think it's sad that most graphic designers still don't get credit for their work. I've always maintained that whatever success and renown I've achieved as a graphic designer is because I'm in an industry—book publishing—that routinely gives credit to its designers. Kids, get your name on what you do. Peace out.

Jessica Helfand

"I am, in principle, morally opposed to hero worship, but I'd like to announce that in my next life, I'd like to be Nigella Lawson." So begins "Time Waits for No Fan," a memorable piece written by Jessica Helfand for the blog Design Observer, the popular forum she cofounded.

Jessica's pieces on Design Observer are among my favorites, not only because they are smart, funny, and erudite, but because her contributions consistently manage to bridge the academic with the arcane and almost always contain a uniquely personal insight. She deftly writes about cooking and creativity, gardening and Greer Allen, the Design Police and the Dixie Chicks. And somehow, when Jessica Helfand writes, I sincerely believe that she is writing directly to and for me. Remarkably, I am only one of her many, many admirers who feel this way.

But successful blogging is only one more recent manifestation of Jessica's abundant talent. A one-time student of Paul Rand, she is a partner in the design firm Winterhouse, an accomplished author, and a critic at the Yale School of Art.

In "Time Waits for No Fan," Jessica contemplates the cult of celebrity fascination. "Fanship, a splinter group of hero worship, is a natural consequence of contemporary life," she writes. Well, truth be told: Jessica Helfand may want to come back as Nigella Lawson in her next life, but in my next life, I'd like to come back as Jessica Helfand.

What was your first creative memory?

I have two. I'm not sure if this counts, but I can remember watching TV and hiding under my parents' bed every time the station identification for CBS appeared, showing the famous "eye" icon designed by William Golden in 1951. I fear that the fact that I responded in terror to a logo says a lot about my career choice.

A few years later—I was probably about 10 or 11 at the time—I was on my way to a birthday party. As we gathered by the door and got ready to leave, my mother handed me the gift, which she'd wrapped rather minimally in plain, brown craft paper. I promptly took off my coat and went to my room to return moments later with a coffee can full of markers. After about ten minutes of channeling my inner Bodoni—lots of letterform, as I recall—I was ready to go to the party. My parents say that's when they knew I was going to be a graphic designer, although I don't think I myself knew until about ten years later.

When specifically did you have that realization?

In high school, I took a six-week intensive summer workshop at The Institute for Architecture and Urban Studies in New York. This was an incredible place—part studio, part think tank—that was a clearinghouse for all sorts of interesting people passing through New York in the 1970s. I remember feeling that life in an office with ugly, overhead fluorescent lamps was unimaginable, but if I could be in a place where people drew all day on drafting tables lit by luxo lamps, then I would always be happy.

Fear of a logo and love of a *lamp*. There's a pathology waiting to be diagnosed here, I'm sure.

Did you ever have serious aspirations to pursue any other type of career?

At one point, I was pretty serious about acting. As an undergraduate at Yale, every minute I wasn't in the studio, I was in rehearsal for something. During the four years, I was in 24 shows, most of them musicals. This was Yale, remember: *lots* of Cole Porter. I'd played the cello for 15 years prior to college, and I'd always been interested in theater, but I have to say that the catalyst came when I had this boyfriend—for maybe 15 minutes—about whom I remember (not surprisingly) *very little* except that he used to sing to me.

And one day I was imitating him, and someone overheard me and pointed out that I had perfect pitch and a three-and-a-half octave range. Hello! Fast forward to an audition, and the next thing I know I'm doing the Judy Holliday role in *Bells Are Ringing*.

Why didn't you pursue acting?

After I graduated, I went to a few auditions, and I grew pretty disillusioned with the prospects. But I wasn't ready to go apprentice in a design studio right away, either. So I got a job reading scripts for a producer. Most of the scripts were so dreadful that one weekend I went home and wrote one myself. I submitted it, got an agent, wrote for daytime television—the only television job besides news in those days—and struggled as a scriptwriter for about three years before realizing that, unlike my colleagues, I had no aspirations to move to Los Angeles, drive a Porsche, and write sitcoms. And I really missed making things. One day I looked over my scripts and was amazed to see how *visual* they were: It was like there was a graphic designer still in me, struggling to break free. I went back to Yale a year later for my MFA, and the rest, as they say, is history.

How would you define the term "graphic design"?

Somehow, I think graphic design succeeds best when it resists definition.

Do you work primarily by hand or with a computer?

Our work at Winterhouse always benefits from drawing, from pinning up our work and drawing right on the wall over it, from sketching not only beforehand but *during* the process. Computers are great, really, but they don't do the thinking for you.

Are you wary of people who can't draw?

I wish I wasn't, but I have to confess that I think I am. Bill [Drenttel, Helfand's husband and partner at Winterhouse] can't draw, and we tease him when he tries to: But he's so gifted in other ways that it's easy to forgive him.

Do you find that you have a process for initiating your design work?

We talk and draw, draw and talk. And argue and disagree. And talk some more.

I also get a lot of ideas while I'm driving. Which is good, because we have two children and I'm always driving them somewhere. I have sketchbooks everywhere—by my bed, in the car—but half the time, the visual ideas I have end up in the margin of the newspaper or on the back of an envelope. In my next life, I'll be more disciplined about where I draw—but I do try to draw as much as possible, and get my students to draw. It's a way to push your visual thinking.

Words don't replace making things—they can't. And I think that having grown up in Paris, and having to speak French in school every day, and playing the cello—its own kind of language— I appreciated, early on, the ability to communicate something quickly, instantaneously. That's what drawing can do and why I have come to believe in it so strongly. It can move an idea along so efficiently. There's a purity to drawing that I find intoxicating.

Do you have an opinion on pre-design research?

I'm resistant to market research and user testing,

even though I recognize and appreciate their benefits from afar. But historical research is an intrinsic part of a lot of our work, and I love it.

When do you know a project is finished?

I don't. This is why I have a partner, and Bill is like a laser beam in terms of focusing on details, whereas I'm impatient and I lose interest. I'm good at starting things—Bill is, too—but I'm not always so good at finishing them. Mostly, though, we tend to have long-term clients and projects, so the goal is less about finishing than it is about sustaining the energy, coming up with new ways to keep the work fresh.

How do you assess your own work?

With great difficulty. Like most designers, I am pretty competitive, but I'm also not so good at being criticized. Being a mother and a teacher—parallel jobs I've come to love and appreciate over the last decade—has made me more critical but also more consistent. As I get older, though, I'm less good at being criticized by others, which is what makes Design Observer [the blog about design and visual culture founded by Helfand, Drenttel, Michael Bierut, and Rick Poynor] sometimes so hard: I find the openness of writing and receiving responses— some of which can be quite harsh—something I'm still getting used to.

If we write too politically, people complain. Too much about graphic (as opposed to other) design, and readers complain. I'm too obtuse one day, too vapid the next. Too abstract and intellectual. Too cultivated. Not cultivated enough. I love blogging, but you can't win. And as a way of assessing your own work, blogs give you a wide open, no-holds-barred access to your audience—for better or worse.

Put another way: I write to figure out what I can't make in the studio; I make work in the studio to try to figure out how to engage bigger ideas about design—the ones I can't quite reach in my writing or get to so directly. And when all else fails, I have a painting studio in my basement that is my true sanctuary.

How do you know when something you've created is good?

It is a balance, and maybe too restrictively so, but I'm happiest when I've made something new, something I never made before, yet that gestures to something for which I'm already known.

So, for example, I was really proud of *Below the Fold*—an occasional journal we write, design, and publish from the Winterhouse Institute. We'd never done this before, something this ambitious that combines writing, editing, using our library, and mining our collections; we collaborate and make work in this way.

But even though *Below the Fold* is a new effort, it's built upon something very familiar in our work: Not familiar in a repetitive, been-there-done-that sort of way, but familiar in the sense that people know that we're big readers, that we write, that we live with 8,000 books. So without overstating it, I like that there's a sort of intentionality, an intellectual appetite underlying the work. And if that's the backstory, *Below the Fold* could go on reinventing itself indefinitely.

Do you keep a journal?

No. But a lot of sketchbooks: one for clients, one for paintings, one for collage and travel. One for my daughter, a collaborative sketchbook that we share, which includes elements of all the above.

Do you feel your education has fundamentally influenced your design ability or would you say that you're more self-taught?

HOW TO THINK LIKE A GREAT GRAPHIC DESIGNER

I am a big believer in education. Actually, I am an even *bigger* believer in a liberal arts education, which is to say that I believe an undergraduate school should provide the broadest education. College is for reading literature and studying language, etc. Art school on top of that is the best possible recipe for living a full life as a designer, because it incorporates both disciplinary breadth in the undergrad curriculum and a kind of critical depth in graduate work that each benefit from the other.

Who is your favorite graphic designer?

I'm a big fan of Ladislav Sutnar. He had an extraordinary gift for balance and grace, an inherent appreciation for a kind of elegant simplicity, and an unmistakable love of theatrical, dimensional scale. Plus, he made mechanicals that were as exquisite as a collage by John Heartfield or Joseph Beuys. And he was versatile—he designed everything, back when there really *was* something graphic about graphic design.

Who has influenced you most in your career as a graphic designer?

First, Bradbury Thompson, who was my teacher— and I was his teaching assistant—at Yale, and who so impressed me by his humanity, his intelligence, and his generosity. There is no one who has impressed me more as a teacher, nor whose skills as an educator have influenced me more. He proved to me you can be a tough critic and still be a sweetheart.

Cleve Gray was a lesser-known yet prolific painter who died in 2004 and was my mentor for the last few years of his life. When I studied painting in grad school, I was told I couldn't paint. Cleve showed me not only that I could paint, but that I *had* to paint. His unwavering devotion to making work every day of his life, and his approach—a blend of focus and forgiveness—have been a *huge* inspiration for me.

I would also have to say I have been, and continue to be, deeply influenced by my partner, William Drenttel—who also happens to be my husband. We met when I was just out of grad school, and he encouraged me, and continues to encourage me, as both a writer and a maker. Bill is an insatiable reader, an enthusiastic force in the studio, and skilled in so many ways I am not. He's got an uncanny instinct about clients. He's gifted three-dimensionally, and he's prescient—he's got a sixth sense about where things are headed, and why. He's a smart, *smart* art director.

Mostly, though, I have been influenced by his generosity: to his employees, past and present, to our suppliers, past and present, to our colleagues and our clients, our family, and me. He loves graphic design, and if and when I waver, he reminds me why I do, too—often by surprising me. It's that simultaneous presence of sustained support coupled with a perpetual element of surprise that make me want to do better work.

Where do you see yourself in five years? What are you doing?

The short answer:
Surviving my childrens' adolescence!
The longer answer:
Healthy and happy.
The detailed answer:
Painting. Making letterpress books in our barn. Teaching. Learning to be a better listener, to be more resilient, to be productive in ways I can't even envision today.

Do you have recurring dreams or nightmares?

I have two: One is that the laundry hasn't been done in 12 years and is piled up to the ceiling, only I can't figure out how to turn the machine on.

The other is that I'm back in graduate school at Yale, being judged by my colleagues on the faculty—with whom I've taught for a decade—and they've decided that the world has changed so much since I received my MFA in 1989 that *I have to do my thesis over again.*

What do you think of the state of contemporary graphic design?

At the moment, I'm extremely disillusioned.

I think style has a way of superceding content, that the rise and proliferation of individual technologies have had a negative effect on human civility; and I think that designers are getting complacent. But that's just today.

I do think that the bigger issue here, with all due respect, is the degree to which graphic design, by its very nature, conspires to lend authority to things that are undeserving. Implicit in this assumption is a set of value judgments that have frequently been raised in the First Things First manifesto: *Somebody's got to design dog food, so why not me?* These are things we think about and talk about constantly in our studio. And our children are aware of it too, and should be: It's not a double standard for us—and our house and studio are attached, making it even more of an issue. We recently designed a milk label for a farmer who couldn't afford to pay us: We get free milk and eggs for life, instead. Something about this transaction made me more aware of pesticides and added hormones. Among other things.

But there are other kinds of social change: I participated in the New York Art Directors Club debate on "Designism," and Winterhouse collaborated with AIGA and the NYU School of Journalism to launch the "Polling Place Photo Project," which was all about the kind of "citizen designer"—or, as

NYU's Jay Rosen would say, the "citizen journalist"—outreach: people using their cell phones to visually document a process, leveraging their right to vote into a project to document their polling places.

It's not much, but it's a start. More and more as time goes on, all of our projects are informed, in some way, by enacting some larger, more comprehensive kind of social change. Interestingly, it seldom comes from a kind of manifesto-like appeal or a subversive effort. Rather, it takes collaboration, coordination, concentration. I'm beginning to think design can be a catalyst for change. It can happen. And should.

Is there anything you dislike about being a graphic designer?

Software upgrades make me anxious, and remind me how little control I have over anything. I keep waiting for Adobe to follow Coca-Cola's lead and bring back Photoshop 1.0.... They could call it "Photoshop Classic," and people over 40 like me would be in heaven.

Seymour Chwast

Seymour Chwast is an elder statesman of the design community and is among the most influential designers and illustrators of our time. Together with Milton Glaser and Edward Sorel, he cofounded the legendary Push Pin Studios in 1954, and became its director when the studio changed its name to The Pushpin Group in the early '80s.

Seymour's design and illustrations have been used in advertising, animated films, corporate and environmental graphics, books, packaging, and record covers. His posters are in the permanent collection of New York's Museum of Modern Art, the Cooper-Hewitt National Design Museum, and the Library of Congress. He was inducted into the Art Directors Club Hall of Fame in 1984, and the American Institute of Graphic Arts gave him its prestigious Medal a year later.

When I e-mailed Seymour the questions I planned to ask him for this book, he replied that he wouldn't tell me about his likes and dislikes because "lists . . . smack of idolatry. I will not tell you what I wear in bed." Instead, Seymour described things that are far more interesting, and a lot less tangible: listening to his conscience, keeping up with the latest trends, and finding unconventional design solutions. He also describes "painting on weekends in the country with a Marx Brothers movie on the tube" and his disdain for rejection.

What was your first creative memory?

> Drawing a lady's head with an eyebrow pencil while waiting for my mother in a beauty parlor.

When you were little, what did you want to be when you grew up?

> A cartoonist working for Walt Disney, partially because I had seen *Snow White* and *Pinocchio*.

When did you realize that you wanted to be a graphic designer?

> In high school in Brooklyn—where my art teacher who emigrated from Germany in the '30s taught us about the great poster designers and forced us to enter every poster competition. At that time, I was introduced to *Gebrausgraphik*, the first graphic design magazine.

What did you study in college?

> At the Cooper Union School of Art, I studied what was called "Advertising Art." I have an honorary PhD in Fine Art from the Parsons School of Design.

How would you define the term "graphic design"?

> Everything that's printed, including illustration, photography, and drawn art for animation.

Do you typically work alone or with other people?

> I work with art directors, entrepreneurs, editors. I design by myself or with my designer.

Do you work primarily by hand or with a computer?

> I draw on paper with my designer executing the drawings, and other work, on a computer.

Do you find that you have a "process" for initiating your design work?

> At first, I search for metaphorical symbols until I find those most appropriate for the project.

Inspiration comes from illustrated books and Google. With an illustration project, I search for the right style or method of execution, which involves looking at the work of others.

How do you know when something you've created is good?

I never know if anything I've created is good, but I know I'm done when I give up looking for other ideas.

How important to your work is writing?

My illustration is a reaction to stories conveyed as words. Sometimes the design problem is described verbally.

Do you feel you are an intuitive designer or are you more intellectual in your approach?

After my mind has done its job, Mr. Hand takes over.

Do you keep a book or files for inspiration?

A file with inspiration is silly when you have a library and computer.

Do you feel that your education has fundamentally influenced your design ability or would you say that you are more self-taught?

Education in the broadest sense—meaning exposure to all aspects of our history and culture—has been vital to my design ability; technique and craft have to be learned as well.

Who has most influenced you in your career as a graphic designer?

Saul Steinberg, André François, Paula Scher, Milton Glaser, Winsor McCay, and Erik Nitsche.

Would you consider your work to be influenced by
contemporary culture?

My work is influenced by culture—especially design and art of 100 years ago—up to but not including the present day.

How much, if any, research do you do before starting
a project?

One should do as much research as necessary.

At a point, I find it useful to let my mind wander and land on something, an unconventional solution.

Tell me about some of the things you like and dislike.

A list of likes and dislikes is very Japanese if you include, "What is your favorite flower and tree?" Lists like this smack of idolatry. I will not tell you what I wear in bed.

Where do you see yourself in five years?

At a drawing table.

Are you afraid of anything?

I am afraid of being exposed.

What is your favorite thing to do?

Play with my dogs. The best thing is painting on weekends in the country with a Marx Brothers movie on the tube.

Do you regret anything?

I regret not going into real estate.

What do you think of the state of contemporary
graphic design?

It's good and bad, as always, but I shouldn't judge because the generational difference makes it hard for me to relate to "contemporary" design.

Do you think graphic designers have any obligation
to create design that inspires social change?

There is no obligation—but we must follow our conscience and human sensibilities.

What do you love most about being a graphic designer?

I love seeing my work in print. I also enjoy seeing other people seeing my work in print.

Is there anything you dislike about being
a graphic designer?

Having to keep up with the latest "trends." And I hate rejection.

Lucille Tenazas

Lucille Tenazas is often referred to as a thinking designer's designer. This is apt, because at the heart of her work is a rigorous exploration of both the magical and the logical, and what she herself describes as a lifelong interest in the complexity of language and the overlapping relationship of meaning, form, and content.

Born and educated in the Philippines, English is Lucille's second tongue. Yet you'd never know this by examining her impressive body of work and the way that she literally paints with language. Her typographic skills are masterful, and her designs examine both the art of communication as well as the mysterious science of verbal and visual messaging.

After spending 20 years working in San Francisco and one year abroad in Rome, Lucille recently relocated to New York. She has returned to the pivotal place where she first started her career and believes that this full circle is particularly appropriate now, since she is more committed than ever to exploring the boundaries between the instinctive and the cerebral, the rational and the abstract.

During our interview, Lucille was animated and entertaining. She was working on her first monograph, so our conversation touched on topics she was investigating for the book. We talked about the formative relationship she had with her father, Michael Bierut's influence, and the significance of growing up in a matriarchal society.

What was your first creative memory?

I think my first creative memory is from the first grade. I was born and raised in the Philippines, in Manila. From kindergarten to college, I went to only one school. It was a Catholic girls' school run by German nuns. What a list of adjectives! Catholics, girls, German nuns. But in the Philippines, it was the only way you could get a good education. It was a single-sex school, so it was either all girls or all boys, and the schools were all run by religious orders. I went to a very good liberal arts women's college that happened to have good arts and science degrees.

I was dying to leave and go to a coed university, but at the time, Manila was under martial law; [Ferdinand] Marcos was in power, and the one university that I had considered going to in order to study fine arts was a very politically active school. Students were being hauled off to prison. They were always out in the street demonstrating, and at that point, my father—he was still alive at the time—said, "You know, you're not really going to get a very good education if you're out there in the streets, so you might as well stay in the school and get a good education." Which I did.

This is all in the context of my first creative memory, which is this: When I was in first grade, I remember being in math class, and we were learning arithmetic. Addition, subtraction, and so forth. I remember we were asked to create visuals, a "two apples plus three apples equals five apples" kind of thing. The teacher told us we could do whatever we wanted to make our own visual representation. I remember using trees.

Now, there's the prototypical tree, which is an iconic trunk with a cloud around it, which everyone uses to represent trees. But I remember that I drew every single kind of tree. I had a palm tree, I had trees with leaves; I had trees with different kinds of leaves, trees with round leaves. It took me a long time to do this. And as we were working, my teacher walked around checking papers and observed our progress. I still remember her footsteps on the wooden floor. She stopped at my desk for what seemed like a long time. All I could think of was, "Why is she stopping next to me? Did I do something wrong?" But then she said to me, "You are a good artist." It was the first time I had received this kind of affirmation. It wasn't required, and it wasn't asked for. And it was my first memory of creativity bolting away from the norm.

Was this the moment you decided to do something creative with your life?

It was a progression. After the first affirmation of my creative talent, I was considered the artist. In elementary school, all eyes would be on me when a teacher would ask, "Okay, who will draw this on the board?" Of course, I would draw it. Or when we had school art contests, the principal would put a little star on the best one on the bulletin board. And invariably, it was always mine. I would look around, and there was always the acknowledgment, "Oh, it's Lucille's work." It was not something to brag about. I looked at myself knowing I was unique and wondering why I had this gift.

My parents saw this, and when I was in the sixth grade, there was a newspaper competition for kids to submit a drawing. The winning drawing would appear in the national paper. And I won it. I would win these awards, and my parents would say, "Oh, submit your drawings for this thing and do this." And I would get the award, like 25 pesos for winning. This became an ongoing thing. There was always some activity I was involved in wherein I would win an award.

Then my father passed away. I was 16 and in high school. Initially, he had planned for me to be something else, a doctor or an architect. But when I stayed up late drawing, my father would stay up and sit with me and watch. I'd sit at the dining table with my crayons and markers all laid out, and he would sit at the head of the table very quietly observing me. Every once in a while, he would lean over and say, "Why did you make this red?" And I would say, "Because I like it." I was so involved in what I was doing that I think I was mostly unconscious of his presence.

In hindsight, his presence meant a lot to me. He didn't say much. He was an engineer, not an artist, but he understood early on that there was a path that I had charted for myself. So when I went to college, it made perfect sense that I would pursue a career in the arts. I knew when I was in high school that I didn't want to be a fine artist; I didn't want to be a painter. I wanted to be a designer.

Since design wasn't a legitimate major in the Philippines, I studied for a bachelor of fine arts. It was quite a good education, though not strictly about graphic design. But my trajectory was pretty clear from the beginning.

Do you think that you have a style to your work?

It depends. On the surface, it's all about typography. But as you look deeper, it starts to unravel. It becomes more layered. Yes. **My work is predominantly typographic, but there is a deliberate marriage of the linguistic element to the visual elements. It is actually more about language than it is about type.**

When I was growing up, I learned English from a very academic point of view. Adherence to this was strictly enforced. When I arrived in the States, I could speak the language and make myself understood, but I was practicing in a profession where language was used as a way to communicate but also as a way to play. So for someone who learned English in a very strict academic mode, this became my time to play.

To me, your work seems to be the product of an equal combination of intuition and intellect.

It is. I've talked about this, how my left brain works with my right brain. When people see my work, or when they hear me speak about my work, they understand the total rationality of what I do. It's very architectural. It's structured, it's a rational progression from "this to this to this." But underlying it all is the sense that I trust my own creative intuition and my judgment. I think this is what makes my work unique. There is a balance.

You've also said that you feel very confident about having the ability to blend the instinctive with the cerebral.

Yes, I do. I think that as one works through one's life, the instinctive and the cerebral become manifested in daily life. I've seen designers whose lives become overchoreographed. They're only wearing black clothes, and their house is immaculate. I don't have that. I don't want it. You can look at my surroundings and see there is an eclectic quality to what's around me. It's carefully chosen, but it's not manufactured.

What do you consider to be manufactured?

Manufactured is unnatural. I can feel it when I first meet someone. I always wonder, "Are they really like this? Is their life so ordered?"

Filipino designers who grew up here have confronted me. They were born and raised here, and when they see me, they tell me that my work doesn't look like a Filipino made it. I tell them that someone with two cultures formed it. And I can't help but wonder what they expected, what they were looking for.

What do you think they're looking for?

I think that they were looking for an old script that is native to the Philippines. Some people don't see this in my work, and they think that's problematic. Other people expect me to be severely monochromatic in my work, and not use tropical colors at all. I tell people that my process can only be arrived at by someone who knows both cultures and both languages. An American designer cannot work like this and cannot think like this simply because they did not go through my experiences.

Do you have a certain process that you go through when you're working?

My process involves a lot of sketching and drawing. Not in an elaborate way—it's more because I don't know how to use the computer, so I don't start out designing on a computer. I think about ideas first and look at the parameters of the project. Sometimes when I look at a problem, there is a solution that's waiting to be tapped. It's very self-evident. So I will try that. But then I move ten steps away from that and reconsider what I can do. Then I go another ten steps away. It may not be literal, but I try and make connections.

When I present the work, I show my client the very rational way the connections have evolved. I start with the self-evident solution and take them on the journey of my thinking. When they see what I see, it's no longer a surprise; it makes perfect rational sense. It's not about, "Why is it red now? Why is it bigger now?" Those minor issues do not have to be dealt with because the client is viewing the bigger picture. That big jump is exponential for them, but the journey gives them the ability to see beyond the tactical and the anticipated.

When you're taking them on this journey, do you do it by displaying a visual record of the process or do you articulate it verbally?

Both. Some people ask me how many layouts I show. Or how many logos I present. Early on in my career—before I lived in California—I lived in New

York. I was 32 and Landor called me in to work on some logos for Saturn. So, I got called in to draw, and I was doing all this work, but I knew they would never go for what I was doing. A few weeks later, there was a whole conference room full of logos, and my work was peppered in. But I knew that they weren't going to go for my work, and that it was a ploy; it was all a ploy to distract and give the client their money's worth. It was bombardment.

That is not the way I work. I would only select a few logos. **I don't show everything. I want the process to be transparent. The process is selective. How can you think if you have a roomful?**

Honestly, can you do that? You can't. You can't concentrate on anything when all four walls are filled up with work.

Did they pick your logo?

No, of course not. I was just there to shake things out a little bit.

How do you know how far to push?

I think that there is a kind of inevitability to my work. I have criteria in my head. Depending on how well I know my client and judging from the interactions I have with them, I determine how much and how far they can be pushed. I pay careful attention to reading the little signals in my interactions. That's why it's really important for me to meet with people. I can read the temperature of the room very well.

How do you think you're able to do that?

It's instinctive. There are times when, after ten minutes, I can experience a level of engagement with a client that is profound. This can only happen if there's a way of addressing them with what they think is important.

I'll share an example with you. About four years ago, I was scheduled to do a lecture in Florida. A young man was assigned to pick me up. He was an older student. He was married. We drove together for 50 minutes—from the airport to the hotel. After that, I never saw him again. He just dropped me off. His job was simply to pick me up from the airport. But we talked about his life and what he thought he should do, and I made some recommendations—that was it.

Two years later, I saw him in Vancouver at the AIGA conference, where I was giving a talk. After I had finished, the young man came up to me. I had forgotten him, and he said, "Do you remember when you gave a lecture in Jacksonville, and I picked you up from the airport?" And I said, "Oh, were you that guy?" And he said, "Your comments changed my life."

Now, I hadn't told him to "do this" or to "do that." I simply asked him to think about what was important to him and to do whatever he could to follow through with it. It wasn't anything more specific than that.

Perhaps this is an overly simplistic way of defining what's important, but I think it's honest. I'm not a marketer spewing clichéd directions for another person. I'm not. For me, our essential purpose is about connecting with another person, another culture, and anyone who is different or has a different life. But our paths and goals are the same. People want to be happy, and they want to have a measure of success and acknowledgment of who they are. Their needs exist regardless of nationality, language, or culture.

We all have similar goals. Once you break that barrier in your encounters, you can make almost every encounter fruitful. I am often asked how I make a connection or how I can enter a boardroom with ten people, mostly men, and understand the temperature of the room and how to gauge it. I try to describe how I can know exactly who the person is in the room that needs to be convinced.

I know it because I can read it. I am very porous and perceptive, and I know that if you ask the right questions, the questions lead to answers and those answers are very revealing and tell you everything you want to know. I think because I'm not an American by birth—I can be very porous.

Another cultural difference that has impacted me is this: The Philippines is a matriarchal society. The concept of feminism didn't take a strong foothold in my country because it was always assumed that women are stronger. It's just not talked about very much. We don't, as you say, have to flex our muscles. But in my family, across the board, though the women are quietly in the background, the men understand that power is evenly distributed. Right now, in the Philippines, women hold many government positions. We even have a woman president. That isn't so easy in the United States.

You recently lived in Rome; how do you feel about coming back to the United States?

New York was really important to me in my development as a designer. When I was first here 20 years ago, I was looking for work, and I remember my first interview with Michael Bierut. At the time, he was working for Massimo Vignelli.

I went on 65 job interviews when I got to New York. I was convinced it would be easier to get a job because I graduated in the winter. I graduated from Cranbrook in December, and I came to New York in January. All this time I was thinking I'd have no competition. But it was a bad time economically in Manhattan, and the city was going through a grave financial slump. It wasn't until the mid-'80s that everybody was high-flying again. But at that time, it was really hard for me to get a job. I remember leaving my portfolio at company after company, showing my work, walking around in the blizzard in the middle of winter and trudging along. Sixty-five interviews to get a job! I think now, coming back after 20 years, I'm older, I'm more mature; it's the same, but it's not the same.

Why so many interviews?

I had a list. When I graduated, Kathy McCoy [then cochair of the design department at Cranbrook Academy of Art] gave me a list and told me where to go. I was green and optimistic, but I got one rejection after another. It wasn't necessarily a rejection because my work wasn't good enough—everyone kept telling me that my work was great, but apparently no one had much work at the time and there weren't many openings. Then Michael Bierut started telling me whom to call, and my list got longer and longer.

I was very diligent about calling these people, and I established strategies for myself. I would tell myself that I was not going to be embarrassed calling someone for the third time in a month. I'd be on the other end of the line, and I'd be so nervous, and I knew I was going to be disappointed: And then the person I was calling wouldn't even take the call. So I became friendly with the receptionists. And then they began helping me out. I'd always try to figure out a way to get someone to talk with me.

One evening, after six o'clock, I called a company I wanted to work for very badly. All the receptionists were gone, so guess who answered the phone? Aubrey Balkind himself. We ended up talking on the phone for an hour, and I knew I could go anywhere if I tried hard enough. And after awhile, I just got shameless.

Did you get a lot of work this way?

Work and connections. After awhile, the number of interviews I had became a joke. People would ask me how many I had and I'd look at my calendar, and I'd say Bierut was number one, and then I had Steff

Geissbuhler, he's number whatever. And the person interviewing me would say, "Gosh, I'm number 55?" They would laugh, and I knew some of the people I was interviewing with were communicating with each other and they'd confer together and ask, "Did you interview the woman from the Philippines who went to Cranbrook?" And they'd compare numbers. So it became a bit of a joke.

Who gave you your first job?

Because of my arrogance, Michael Bierut was my first interview. My second interview was with a small design firm that had opened a year before. I had never heard of them. The company was Harmon, Kemp. Marshall Harmon and David Kemp. I interviewed with them, and they offered me a three-month job working on a project for International Paper. But I was a snob and I thought, "Three months! I want a full-time job!" So I never called them back.

Later that year, I got a call from the recruiter Chris Edwards. Chris asked me if I was still looking for work, and when I told him yes, he told me about two gentlemen who were looking for a designer— and he thought it would be perfect for me. I asked him the name of the company, and when he told me Marshall Harmon and David Kemp, all I said was, "Oh shit." But he pushed me to call them, as they now had a full-time position.

So I called them up and ate crow, and Marshall told me that I should never say no to the little guys. He chastised me. But I got the job, and I worked there for four years. Now, people always ask me about the work that I was doing at Harmon, Kemp. Ellen Lupton told me I was doing work at Harmon, Kemp that no one else was doing. And I had no idea that this particular time in my life would be one of the most fertile periods of my career. But Marshall Harmon and David Kemp were the ones who propelled me. They gave me a chance.

Years later, I was offered a job in San Francisco, and I thought it might be a good thing to do. I was single and mobile, and I figured if I did it once already, I could very well begin again. And that is still my attitude today. Now I'm back in New York after living in Rome. I'm 53, and I realize that I came to this country when I was 25 years old. The number of years I've been here is nearly equal to the number of years that I lived in the Philippines. Now I have an affinity for each culture and for each country. I find it's a wonderful combination. And I can use both backgrounds in my work.

What do you think your life will be like five years from now?

I would like to be in a position where I can still make good work and still produce a good product. I'd like my work to have wide-ranging and wide-reaching repercussions. I don't know what it will be, I just know that I can't operate status quo. I won't work in another office; I can't do that.

I wonder if after over 20 years of working, can I still have a profound influence? I've come back to the States, and I know that the cumulative effect of what I've gone through has changed and altered my work. My work has evolved and has become a product of what I've done. I don't know what the manifestation of it will be. In many ways, I find it incredibly exciting. It is hard but exciting. And worth it.

Vaughan Oliver

Name an iconic song, and I can tell you everything else that was occurring in my life at the time it was popular: Meat Loaf's "Paradise by the Dashboard Light," for example, had me driving a bronze Pinto, sporting yellow flip-flops, and arguing about the effectiveness of Jimmy Carter's cabinet.

These remembrances are frozen in time—I have but a scant memory of what might have come before or after, and I find that I can't recall experiences with the same zeal without the benefit of their musical accompaniments. The song plays, and time slows and then stops as this still-tangible reality pushes forth. The music is as much a part of the memory as the memory is of identity.

Such is the case with the designs of Vaughan Oliver, particularly the hugely influential work he did at 23 Envelope and v23, the studios he cofounded in the 1980s. At these firms, Vaughan created seminal album covers for the British independent record label 4AD and musical artists including the Cocteau Twins, Modern English, This Mortal Coil, and the Pixies. His work with these artists ushered in an unprecedented era of graphic revolution, and his indisputably unique style has influenced subsequent generations of designers eager to redefine the discipline of design and its possibilities.

In our interview, Vaughan reflected on his legendary beginnings, the recent changes in the music business, and his struggles with self-doubt.

[*Oliver begins mid-sentence…*]

I get stuck in my little mind when I'm left to my own devices.

What happens when you get stuck in your own little mind?

Oh, I think the anxiety increases. Feelings of self-doubt.…

Do you have a lot of feelings of self-doubt?

Oh, don't we always, us creative people? Sometimes you're on top of the world, and other days, you feel worthless and wonder what you've done and what you're doing.

What do you do when that happens? How do you manage to crawl out of that?

Quite simply, I go for a walk. I like green. We have a beautiful, common green [park] that I'm still exploring ten years later. I enjoy that. Rather more than the public house [pub]; the public house can only lead you further into self-doubt.

In what way?

It can go either way, in terms of changing your chemistry. I think it can suspend the self-doubt for a few hours. Then you're back to it.

Do you think that self-doubt helps the creative process in some way?

Not mine. I used to suffer a lot less in the old halcyon days in the 1980s and 1990s, when I had a deadline every day. At the time, I had two assistants, and I was working in the offices of 4AD, where I was doing a lot of work. There was a lot of activity around me, and the deadlines were relentless. The creativity was relentless. There was less room for self-doubt. We were on a roll. And it wasn't only me; it was a period in time when we were blessed with the right juxtapositions of social, cultural, and artistic influences. After punk and post-punk, along with the great blossoming of design awareness, independent record labels and independent designers were flourishing.

When do you think that period ended?

It seemed to dip—to me personally, I don't know about other people—around the mid-'90s. And if I can speak specifically, the music business changed a lot in that period. The adventurous independents were consumed by the majors. And the majors were increasingly run by accountants, who managed to throw out the men with the record collections. I think, generally speaking, that all of the budgets changed. The whole industry changed around that time.

Also, for a person who is not running a business with other people—and I'm not the only one—it's been an unusual period adapting to the technology. I don't mind talking about this 20 years later, as I am still adapting to it. But I expected to be able to relax a little bit, in terms of the effort that I put in.

And have you found that you can't?

No, I can't. It's a kind of different world now, in terms of income, etc. I probably earn about 30 percent of what I used to in the '90s.

Do you feel that's a result of the technological changes, or do you feel like that's a result of cultural changes?

I think it's a combination. I don't think it's one or the other. Again, there are a number of changes. The whole thing seems to have shifted away from the likes of myself, the disempowered.

How do you feel that you're disempowered?

I think it's the disempowerment that fuels self-doubt. I don't know, it's—maybe it's just me. Maybe I just feel less wanted. I still have a relationship with 4AD; but again, their budgets were cut to a minimum. So

I'm working for less than I was getting ten years ago. So I've got to do a job more quickly.

But personally speaking, I've struggled because I never had a business partner. And I'm not naturally active in that way. I'm ambitious creatively, but I've never been ambitious business-wise. Whereas my 15, 16 years of business at 4AD fed me creatively and satisfied me creatively. I was cocooned; I never got out. I never networked or met people. I think I suffer from that. Why have I started off on this thread?

[*Laughter.*]

It's the end of the week, and I would like some money for the weekend, please.

I've never felt comfortable about myself or my work. I was brought up just the opposite: If you spoke about yourself, you were being too bold. And one should always show curiosity about the other half of the conversation.

So you basically wait for people to come to you and say, "We need your genius…"

They less frequently do, really. So I'm not very active in finding new business, I've never really been good at it. 4AD still feeds me music, whether it's Scott Walker, or, more recently, TV on the Radio. That moves me. I still want to work with these people and want to make them happy with the packages for their music. If you're still turned on by it, I don't think age is a boundary to your involvement.

Let's talk about how you work. Do you feel that you're more of an intuitive designer, or more intellectual and formal in your approach?

I'd like to think there's a little bit of both. I'd like to think that there are ideas and concepts behind what I do and why I start projects. But often when I start to explain those ideas or concepts, folks find them bizarre or banal, and they aren't always immediately recognizable.

How do you get people to understand them?

I make some pictures. And speak thoughtfully about their work. I'm speaking specifically about the music business here, although my work is much broader. I think we work very idiosyncratically, intuitively, and organically. It might be one word on an album that sets it off. The ideas are in that word. I try to describe the tone and the textures and the atmosphere of the music.

I said somewhere recently that we were not interested in reaching the audience—and in retrospect, that was an untrue thing to say. But first and foremost, I am keen on satisfying the musicians, for whom I invariably have great respect. But graphic design is nothing if it doesn't communicate.

While words like "mystery" and "ambiguity" can be used to describe our work, that work still needs to communicate a message.

I think our work has been successful because we leave it open. We're not trying to define anything. But at the same time, we're not just settling for the bandwidth like, "This is the signifier you get from their clothes and their hair, and the way they hold their instruments." I would like to think there's a deeper imagination that is brought to bear.

Imagination is an old-fashioned word, but I still believe in it. It's an old-fashioned term, like "care" and "quality." Old-fashioned values and things are still at the heart of what we do.

Did you always want to be a graphic designer?

When I left school, I thought, "I want to work in art." I loved music and record sleeves—it was as simple as that. And I thought the best way to achieve this was to study graphic design.

I originally thought about pursuing fine art but immediately reconsidered. I couldn't help but wonder how many painters make a living at the end of the day. There was a practical side to me, and I needed to make a living. Let's not forget that I am a working-class boy from the Northeast! I had no real contacts in business and no real understanding of where one could go from a fine-art curriculum; I thought, "Graphic design can lead to a job."

And I remember turning up for an interview at the college in my school uniform, with a tie, sweater, and the school badge on the blazer. The interview room was in the space where people met for coffee. After seeing all the paint splattered over the halls and 3D hairdos, I felt so straight!

I remember going into the interview and being asked what graphic design meant. And that morning, I'd been wise enough to reach for the dictionary and just reiterated what I'd read there: That design was intended for mass reproduction. Then the interviewer wanted me to expand on that, and all I could do was repeat it.

So I didn't have any notion of what graphic design really was. I didn't dare say I wanted to design record sleeves; that wasn't a potential profession in those days. All through college, I focused on illustration; I saw it as a means of personal expression in the commercial world. I actually avoided design. In fact, the only graphic designer I'd heard of after three years of college was Milton Glaser. I didn't really have a fascination for graphic design and its history.

I left college under a cloud; it was very disappointing. And I applied for jobs locally, but no one was interested. I was a small-town boy; I didn't really want to go to London—I resisted for a long time. I applied for the police force. I was delivering bread. I wanted to do anything but what I seemed obliged to do. I came to London and couldn't get a job in illustration after two weeks. Rather than get a bad job, I moved into design; and slowly things began to take off.

So this was something that happened naturally for you, in terms of your ability to practice graphic design? Did you ever feel like you had to struggle to understand how to do this?

Initially, yes. The first piece of artwork I put together for 4AD was the first piece of artwork I put together, ever.

So how did you know it was good?

I didn't. In terms of developing art that was practical for print, I needed a lot of conversations with the printer to prepare the work correctly.

But what about the aesthetic?

How do I know when it's right? That's a good question: How do you know when it's right? How do you know when to stop? You just do. You just do. I think it's a combination of being satisfied and the client being satisfied. That's generally where I'd stop. More often than not, in those early days, I was full of wanting to change things, and I wanted to do something different. I wanted to go against the grain. I suppose I am a punk at heart, even though I didn't have a punk aesthetic. But I found I was generally at loggerheads with the bands I was working with. They would constantly tell me: "This is what we need. This is what we should have." But I was showing them things that they hadn't seen the likes of before.

We were trying to do record sleeves that didn't look like record sleeves, and we had to believe in what we were doing if we were going to get anyone else to believe it, too.

I remember one day—I think I was working on the first Modern English album—I was designing a photograph within a border, with a nice bit of type centered at the top and a nice bit of type at the bottom. And I recall one of the senior designers saying, "That's more like it! It looks more like a record sleeve." At that point, I'd done something wrong. I knew I'd done something wrong. It looked predictable. That's not what I was after.

You said that you were at loggerheads with some of the bands. I find that interesting, given where we started the conversation. You felt very strongly you wanted to do something different. What gave you the courage to do that?

Well, just the very opposite of self-doubt. Being bullish. I think at the end of the day, I always wanted to take the work further. It's not that I had particularly strong persuasive powers. In those days, I didn't know how to sell a job. But I always had ambitions for my work to be timeless.

Sometimes I'll look back and I'll see certain package designs that I've done, and I think there are some that look dated, and then something changes, and suddenly it's classic. And then, after a certain amount of time, it becomes timeless, accepted, and beloved. But I always think there's that pain barrier before it morphs into that.

What do you think about the music industry right now?

I'm not sure I'm qualified to say, but I think it's in a sad predicament. There is a lack of rebelliousness and surprise. I also see this in students. I think we're going through a period where the concept of a young person being rebellious is unusual. I think we're going through a period where students in the U.K. are going to college not for an education but to get a job. And I see staff-to-student ratios of 1 to 100. One staff to 100 students—I find that shocking.

How do you see yourself in the future? What will make you the happiest?

What would make me happiest? I would like to get back my love for graphic design, because I think I've lost it. I don't want this to sound like a lament for the olden days, but I find that working on a drawing

HOW TO THINK LIKE A GREAT GRAPHIC DESIGNER

board with a parallel motion and having a scalpel with a comma on the end of it—and placing that comma into a filigree list with a bit of type—was very satisfying. I found that there was a physical and mental connection between my brain, my heart, and down my arm; I had a degree of precision, with a tool, and I had a sense of craft. And that's what I miss, really, that sense of craft. I miss having physically done a day's work at the end of a day.

But again—it doesn't have to be one or the other. There are so many fantastic things about the computer that I enjoy. But a question about how much I enjoy work is also connected to where I am in life and the kinds of things I've gone through and how much confidence I have. It is easy to lose confidence when things implode. And the designer thrives on confidence. For me, it's just seeping back.

Steff Geissbuhler

I first met Steff Geissbuhler in 2005, the night he was honored with the American Institute of Graphic Arts' Medal for his sustained contribution to design excellence and the development of the design profession. As crowds of well-wishers clamored around to congratulate him, he was humble and gracious. These are only a few of the accomplishments and qualities that define this influential and inspiring practitioner.

Steff is among the most important designers of brand and corporate identity programs in the world. Before launching C&G Partners, he was a principal at Chermayeff & Geismar for 30 years. He has worked for a broad spectrum of international and national clients, creating printed materials for Philip Morris, the Alvin Ailey American Dance Theater, and Morgan Stanley. He designed the venerable identity for NBC, a new identity system for the New York Public Library, and environmental signage for the IBM building in Manhattan.

While Steff's influence on our visual culture is vast, design also runs deep in his family's roots: His grandfather was an architect, his mother created tapestries, and his godfather was a lithographer. Still, Steff is a thoroughly modern designer, both in scope and in style. His work is single-minded, telegraphic, and utterly timeless.

What was your first creative memory?

I couldn't tell which was the first, but I'm sure it had something to do with exploring and discovering, whether it was the architecture in a leaf, a wooden block balancing on another, or forming a shape in the sandbox without a "form." I have this 1949 calendar, which I created in kindergarten at the age of six, where we glued, stitched, and drew on each page to represent each month. Most of it was sort of predetermined—a snowman in January, a flowering tree in May, and apples in September. However, there were individual variations in how you cut, pasted, or colored-in things. I can still smell the glue.

When you were young, what did you want to be when you grew up?

A soldier, a butler, a cowboy, and an Indian chief. However, I did not want to be any of these things when I grew up—I wanted to be them then.

When did you realize that you wanted to be a graphic designer?

At about age 15. The posters hanging all over Switzerland appealed to me, made by designers like Celestino Piatti, Herbert Leupin, Armin Hofmann, Hans Erni, Herbert Matter, and others.

Did you ever have serious aspirations to pursue any other type of career?

Music. I played the cello for 12 years and the upright bass in a jazz quintet. But I found that playing gigs on weekends was starting to hinder me in drawing because my fingers would be swollen when I held the charcoal on Monday morning. Also, my cello teacher asked me once how many cellists were recording in the world. When I couldn't answer with more than five names, I realized that I wasn't going to be good enough, and it dampened my ambitions as a musician. That didn't stop my kids from later calling me "Yoyo Pa."

What did you study in college?

I studied graphic design at the Allgemeine Gewerbeschule in Basel, Switzerland, for six years and graduated with a diploma equivalent to an MA here in the U.S. My education in Basel has definitely influenced my thinking more than anything else.

Do you work primarily by hand or with a computer?

Both. A lot of sketching happens away from the computer, in sketchbooks, on snips of paper, the backs of envelopes, etc. The computer then becomes a production tool, where alternative versions can be quickly generated and variations can be explored.

Some ideas, however, are directly generated with the computer, because they cannot be sketched, due to their complexity and the mechanics of their construction.

Do you find that you have a process for initiating your design work?

Yes, it's called research. I learn about the client as much as I can, understand the problem from the ground up, who the competition is, who the audience is. Then comes thinking and doodling, exploring the visual potential, and always with a consideration of what the media is, making sure of the design's functionality and appropriateness.

When starting a project, how do you feel emotionally?

I want this project to be the best I ever did. I want it to be different, groundbreaking; I feel very charged. The closer I get to a presentation, the more anxious I get, especially if I'm not convinced that I have yet found *the* solution.

When do you know a project is finished?

A project is finished when the client is happy and paid-up.

*How do you know when something you've created
is good?*

> When it performs as it was meant to. When it's
> new and different. When the client is coming back
> for more.

How confident are you in your own judgment?

> I trust my own judgment, but then again, I usually
> show the work to my partners to check. That's why
> I have partners, rather than being a solo designer.

*Can you tell me about a project that was going badly
that you turned around? How did you rescue it?*

> I honestly can't remember any projects that fit
> that description. All of the projects that went badly
> under my watch kept going sour until they were
> just too bad, beyond repair, or lost. In most cases,
> it has to do with bad chemistry between the client
> and myself. However, I can remember a few situa-
> tions where the client complained to me about
> oversights, repeated typos, or misspellings, or an
> attitude problem by an employee of mine. In all
> these situations, I believe it was my fault for not
> watching over it or not being involved enough and
> assuming that other people would be careful, con-
> siderate, and attentive. I "rescue" these scenarios
> by paying personal attention and inserting myself
> in the minute details of the process—or by doing
> it myself.

How important to your work is writing?

> Writing is a very important part of my work, in
> the proposal, e-mail, and presentation; in writing
> or rewriting copy; and in describing a project for
> a publication after it's done. I'm jealous of people
> who can express themselves really well with the
> written word.

*Do you feel you are an intuitive designer or are you
more intellectual in your approach?*

I find that a difficult question to answer. Perhaps I'm an "intuitive intellectual" designer.

Intuition plays a large role in my work and has rarely let me down. I often intellectualize my work after the fact.

Is there a favorite place, thing, or person from which you draw inspiration?

My wife.

Who is your favorite graphic designer?

A. M. Cassandre.

Why?

A. M. Cassandre was the ultimate poster designer—he knew exactly how to use scale, perspective, focus, and color to express the essence of the message. He was one of the few painters who created and understood the power of the poster and, with that, created the profession we now call "graphic design." His formal ideas have never lost power and grab me to this day. He made typography an integral part of the image. He translated the essence of a thing—like a train, a ship, or a person—to the most "graphic" expression. Actually, I could say pretty much the same things about Armin Hofmann. Other favorite graphic designers of yesterday and today: Toulouse-Lautrec, Alphonse Mucha, Lucian Bernhard, Wolfgang Weingart, Pierre Mendell.

Who has influenced you most in your career as a graphic designer?

Armin Hofmann has definitely influenced me more than anybody else.

How so?

He showed me how to discover visual ideas by exploring form and color relationships. He showed me the evolution of a thinking process through sketching, rather than just thinking. He instilled a confidence in me to always find a solution to a visual problem. He made me look and see. He has a wonderful sense of humor, and I feel very close to Armin and Dorothea, his wife, as soul mates, even though we speak maybe only twice a year these days.

What is your favorite typeface?

Right now, it's Interstate. Tomorrow, it might be The Sans. I always loved Helvetica and Univers in all cuts, weights, and slants. I can't help it, I'm Swiss!

What do you think of the state of contemporary graphic design?

It's a very exciting time for us graphic designers, because our projects get more and more complex and challenging, and the field of design is getting wider and wider.

What do you think of Ken Garland's 1964 First Things First manifesto?

I'm totally in support of the First Things First manifesto and consider it one of the most important critical writings in design. I'm lucky to have had the opportunity to work with many humanitarian, cultural, and not-for-profit clients as well as cause-related projects. We are not involved in commercial advertising and rarely do product branding; however, the points of the manifesto apply to all design work and designers. We all have to make choices.

What do you think of the First Things First 2000 manifesto?

It was an important revisitation of the original. I'm not sure, however, how much change both of these manifestos caused in actual attitude and intellectual approach. Money keeps on winning.

*What do you think of Milton Glaser's "12 Steps on the
Road to Hell"? What number have you crossed?*

I had the fortune to never have had to do any of the
exact things Milton is listing. However, I designed
for many years the annual report for a cigarette
manufacturer, for example, but the same company
also sponsored my posters for New York City's
cultural affairs events and the visual identity for
the Alvin Ailey American Dance Theater. I certainly
danced a few rounds with the devil in my career,
and he often took the lead.

Stephen Doyle

Stephen Doyle is principal and creative director at Doyle Partners, a New York–based studio known for its eloquence in all things graphic design. Previously an art director for Tibor Kalman at M&Co, as well as a member of the art departments at Rolling Stone *and* Esquire, *Stephen is comfortable working in numerous media for a stunning variety of clients. To wit: He was the founding creative director of the irreverent* Spy *magazine and also developed the brand identity for K-Mart's line of Martha Stewart Everyday products. He often cites fine art as an inspiration for infusing his design with a sense of humanity and personal engagement.*

For our conversation, Stephen gave me the option of interviewing him either in his office or at the home he shares with his wife, Gael Towey, the chief creative officer of Martha Stewart Living. I chose to meet him at his Greenwich Village townhouse, and though I was both excited and intimidated by the idea of being in the home of such a power couple, my worries were unfounded. A warm and engaging family greeted me; they laughed as they prepared their dinner, and they were genuinely down-to-earth.

Over a bottle of marvelous wine, Stephen and I talked about why he feels his design work is reductive, why he doesn't believe in perfect, and the notion of art as a "fearless perch."

What was your first creative memory?

It was in French class in grade school, when it occurred to me that I wanted to be an architect. One of our projects was to design a house as a way of getting kids to learn the words for house, door, window, and other architectural elements. The house I drew was different from everybody else's. It was a big, modern house, with glass all around and a big, leaning ceiling. I remember experiencing a feeling of elation at the idea of being able to make something different from what everybody else made.

Really?

It distinguished me in some way, in a different currency. I wasn't the tallest kid, I wasn't the smallest kid, but even at a really early age, I realized imagination could differentiate me.

How did people react to this piece of art you created that was so different from everybody else's? Were you given a lot of compliments? Did people think you were weird?

Well, I got an "A" in French! No, nobody thought it was weird. That is my earliest memory, so I don't remember many of the social dynamics of the time. Michael Bierut may remember his fourth-grade French class better than I.

I remember around about eighth grade— or when you get into that phase of puberty when you are very awkward and very unsure of yourself— I was allowed to have a special place in class by being the kid who could draw or the kid who was creative. I wasn't athletic, so I wasn't distinguishing myself in that way. But even the athletic kids respected me because I had this special talent. And it was nice to have something that was respected, something different from everyone else's abilities. Because the usual talents in high school are sports and brains.

Now do you still feel that the talent you have
is special?

Absolutely. We were just at a big family party, and I was sitting next to one of my sisters-in-law, and she said, "You know, Mike [my brother-in-law] thinks you're really cool." Mike's a banker, but he thinks I'm cool because I get to work with David Byrne, and the strangeness of the things I'm exposed to earn me a special place in his heart.

When you had that experience in your French class,
did you know from that moment on that you wanted
to utilize that special power as your vocation? Or was
this something that came later?

I didn't know much about "vocation" then, but I did dream about being an architect. I realized at a very early age that I was willing to sell my soul to the devil to be creative.

Really?

Yes. Once I felt what that felt like, I knew that was where I wanted to go. I didn't know how to go about it, I didn't know anything about careers in the arts at that time.

Did you think you wanted to be a painter?

I did want to be a painter. I took art classes, but I wasn't a very good painter. Though I did work hard at it. When I was in high school, I read *Julius Caesar*, and my copy of the book had a beautiful drawing of Julius Caesar on the cover. It featured a big splotch of red where Caesar was stabbed. I looked on the back of the book and it said: "Cover design by Milton Glaser." At that moment, I felt that Milton Glaser was a on par with William Shake-speare and Julius Caesar, and it was all because of this cover. I think I knew then that there was a way to access this world, but at the time I still didn't know what that was.

So when did you know that you wanted to be a "designer"?

When I came to New York to go to school at Cooper Union, I enrolled in all of the painting classes, but I kept getting kicked out because the teachers were abstract expressionists, and they wanted their way of painting to be honored. And it didn't make any sense to me to be painting that way in the '70s. I was pursuing a very different kind of narrative art. And they didn't get it. One by one, I got kicked out of the classes there. It's a small school, so I was running out of classes to take and finally decided I would have a go at design.

I started doing work in my design class that was humorous—which is what I was doing in the painting classes that didn't go over well—and the teachers were amused by it. They encouraged me, because they saw it as a particular design voice. And as soon as that happened, I knew this was the world for me, because teachers weren't threatened by the design that I was making just because it wasn't serious. It was taking itself seriously, but it had a kind of a humanism and a humanity and wit about it that didn't threaten them.

What do you love most about design?

I love that design is a way to translate a language for an audience. It's a way to interpret words and messages and stories and narratives and ideas, and put them in front of people in a way that makes it easier for them to understand. It's a language and it's a currency. That sounds so serious!

I also love that design gives you an opportunity to be constantly learning. I feel like my entire career is graduate school for me, because I learn about all different kinds of businesses. And I get to understand it to the degree that I can translate it for other people. I think that learning keeps you young and vital and engaged. I can't wait to get to work every day. I could take another 20 minutes with the newspaper, but I love to go there and do what I do with the people with whom I'm doing it. I have a small studio—we're just 10 or 11 people—so we get to choose who we work with very carefully.

Do you turn down a lot of work?

We do. And that's the best part. Because by turning down work, I can work with people who I want to work with and do the work that I think needs to be done.

What kind of work do you turn down?

Our policy is to try to turn down everything unless we're the only people who could do the job really well. If it's a graphic design job and somebody else could do it, there's no point in us getting involved. There's a trajectory in our office that's about literacy and literateness and humanity and social responsibility, and a lot of that work nobody else can do. That's why we do it.

When you say that nobody else can do it, what do you mean? What is it about your studio that makes you specifically so appropriate to do that kind of work?

There's a kind of academic literacy about us and our approach. We have a very language-oriented approach to most problems, so it's about honing language and presenting visuals that reinforce that. It's about projects that need humanity. We're not imagers; we don't do work in the world of fashion. We do a lot of retail work that's about positioning, like the Barnes & Noble logo, and environmental work that determines the typographic vocabulary in a store. The packaging we've done for Martha Stewart is all about engaging the reader and instilling a type of magnetism to the package that helps explain what's in it. It explains the mystique. It's a very literal mystique, but it's also very friendly and tasteful.

How do you know when something you've created is
well-designed?

I know that something's well-designed when it makes my mouth water.

You have an actual, physical reaction?

A physical, visceral, Pavlovian reaction to this thing. There's some connection between seeing and tasting for me.

So your mouth waters, and then you know it's good.

Yes, I can feel it, and I can taste it. It's physical.

Does that happen with all the jobs that you do?
Do you wait for the moment when that happens,
so you know a project is complete?

No, they don't all make me salivate. There's a moment when I'm working on something with my team, and I feel the work transcend. Sometimes the hair stands up on your arm. Then I make copies, and I bring it home to show Gael and the kids, and I go, "Hey, check this out!" And they're like, "Yeah, you're right." We all know something's going on that wasn't there before. We feel it. And there's usually not a whole lot of disagreement.

Everything we do is not excellent, certainly. I don't know that there are many people who can continually produce excellence. The fun is trying to do it. When you're a kid, it's the making of the tree house that's the delight; it's not having the tree house at the end. Once something is produced, I'm so uninterested in it.

Really?

I can't stand it. It's old. The project that I'm currently working on, the problem that I haven't yet cracked— that really entertains me.

*Do you see the end result of your work as producing a
solution to a problem?*

No, it's a process of finding a solution, and that is
what's exciting. Very often you start out with an
idea, then you chase it, and you push it, and you go
all the way around the world, and you come right
back next door to where you started. But it's only by
proving that circle that you know what's vital. And
as you get old like me, sometimes you can do that
loop quicker and quicker.

*Do you find that you often have instant solutions for
design problems?*

Yes.

*How often are they instant and how often are
they labored?*

When *The New York Times* calls and asks if I can do
an Op-Ed piece, I try to do it on the phone with the
art director right then and there. If I've begun to
crack it, then I know I can spend the time on it. But
if I can't find a wedge, or a place to put a wedge in,
or a crack in the problem, then I'll pass. I don't have
the time to chase. I find that I've become a "meeting
thinker." I can generate all kinds of ideas in a meeting when there's an audience. I find that I can really
think on my feet, and it's easier than thinking alone.

What do you think gives you that ability?

Foolhardiness, fearlessness, humor. I could never
make myself that vulnerable if I wasn't able to mess
around with the client and get out of all kinds of
scrapes with a sense of humor.

*What do you think gives you your sense of fearlessness?
What does that come from?*

Experience and a measure of craftsmanship. I know
how to make things with my hands. I had a really
good education and learned how to make things.

As a result, I'm unafraid of solving problems with my hands. And I'm not afraid of getting in over my head with the execution. I know that anything can be done.

Where do you think your sense of verbal fearlessness comes from?

I have no idea. But I can tell you that when I begin to talk this way, even the kids in my studio pull back and start to look at me funny.

Who would you say has most influenced you in your design career?

I've had a lot of mentors. I guess the first biggest influence was an art teacher in high school. I went to a Jesuit high school outside of Baltimore, and he helped me to think of art as a fearless perch.

Really? How did he do that?

By not being a perfectionist. I try to make things really good, and then I try to make something else. I don't ever try to make anything perfect. In fact, I don't believe in perfect. I believe in really good. I believe in a handmade object that retains evidence of its handmade-ness. And that, by nature, is never perfect. As designers, we don't make "just one thing." One project is not the end of the world, and it's not the only thing to be made. A painting is just a painting, and there are more paintings. And you have to make many to begin to make good ones, even though I never accomplished that.

The work that I do, some people think it's precious, some think it's not so precious. I recently read on Armin Vit's Web site Brand New a discussion about the Martha Stewart logo that we just redesigned. The last time I checked, there were 48 entries with comments such as, "The weights of the stems are a little bit uneven....." And so forth. I could not believe how much time people have on their hands to make comments like these!

The purpose of doing the logo the way we did was to create a logo that was a bit imperfect. That is what Martha Stewart is all about, the hand-made effect.

Tell me about some of your influences.

In college, George Sadek was the dean of the art school and a design teacher at the time. He was a huge influence on me, because he delighted in a sense of lunacy and pushing things to their illogical extreme, and that was right up my alley.

Do you think that you push things to their "illogical extreme"?

Yes. Logic—you know where logic will get you:

Logic will get you nowhere. But imagination has the opportunity to rescue you from the quicksand of logic.

You could be a banker with logic. To be a designer, you have to find a new language. You've got to find new colors. You have to surprise people. You've got to make things that are magnetic to humans who don't like design.

Does anything scare you in the area of graphic design or creativity?

No.

Are you insecure about anything in your practice?

Yes, I'm insecure about whether I'm good enough or hip enough or up-to-date enough, or whether my ideas are old-fashioned—all that sort of stuff at any given time.

What do you do in response to that?

I go for a bike ride or swim and then I get back to work. There's nothing to do about it. As a creative person, you have to constantly question whether you're pushing hard and far enough to be creative.

I keep wondering—since I already sold my soul to the devil—whether he's actually coming through for me. I wonder if my work is crazy enough.

How do you think you've sold your soul to the devil?

The deal was that he could have my soul when I died if I could be creative for my lifetime.

What did the devil look like?

[*Laughter.*]

He wasn't there in person. It was conceptual.

Who else influenced you at Cooper Union?

At Cooper—after George Sadek—I studied with Milton Glaser, which was astonishing. He taught editorial design with Henry Wolf. And the greatest thing about that class was that they never agreed on a single thing. It was so validating for me. I was always the intellectual troublemaker in the design classes, and it was incredibly validating to learn that there is no right and wrong. Even Milton Glaser and Henry Wolf couldn't agree on certain principles. So their disagreement was incredibly freeing to me. It was a profound delight. This is why I'm not a scientist. In science, there is a right and a wrong. In design there isn't. It's all quicksand. It's just a different quicksand.

When you're commissioned for a project, how do you begin?

I interview the clients. I've got to understand what the problem is from their point of view. And then you have to not believe them.

Why?

They are the client, and they see it through their own filter. And I always imagine myself as their audience. And luckily, in much of the work that we've done, I usually am. I'm saying "I," but it's the whole studio. I'm not a sole operator, and I would never want to be. When we did *Spy* magazine, we were the kids who would want to read a magazine like that. And now that I'm a 50-year-old guy at the head of a company, I believe that there is an appropriateness about the type of work that we feel suited to do. Again, I also ask: Can we do what nobody else can? Can we associate at least with the audience? Are we the audience?

What happens after the interviews?

I think we're better at hearing than we are at designing.

Really? What do you mean by that?

This is where creativity comes from: being able to deconstruct what people say and find the words in it and blow it back up again. We take paragraphs and slogans and presentations and chip away at them. And then we bring it all back to life. Our design work is reductive. We're more like stone carvers. A big block of stone comes in, and we start chipping away at it until we find the sculpture inside. Some designers are additive. They'll add and layer things on. To me, this is decorative rather than reductive. I would rather uncover the essence of what is already there. All we ever do with the material our clients give us is take things away. We take things away until we can see what is in front of us.

Abbott Miller

An artist, designer, author, curator, and a true intel-
lect, Abbott Miller is a Renaissance man nonpareil.
He is an eloquent advocate and interpreter of design,
and he has spent much of his career investigating the
complex, multifaceted relationship between graphic
design and written language in our culture.

    As editor and art director of the luminous arts
magazine 2wice, *Abbott creates with both words and*
pictures, demonstrating a singular fluency in the two
disciplines. The magazine, like all of Abbott's work,
engages readers with an aesthetic framework that is
heavily invested with meaning, thought, and the bliss
evoked by the finely crafted image. He is comfortable
designing for an unusually diverse range of material,
from the Russian avant-garde to Money *magazine*
to artist Matthew Barney's edgy Cremaster Cycle.

    With their flair for integrating content and
form, Abbott and his wife, Ellen Lupton, pioneered
the concept of "designer as author" through their
efforts in the firm Design/Writing/Research. Sensing
that the design field lacked the critical analysis of
realms like architecture, they began to amass a body
of criticism—some collected in the book Design
Writing Research—*that has helped us to better*
understand the practice and ideas of graphic design.

    In our interview, Abbott regaled me with hilar-
ious tales of childhood, discussed the inspiration he
gets from his wife and his Pentagram partners, and
recalled an early writing assignment for Steven Heller.

Do you have a recollection of your first
creative memory?

Well, this is scatological, but I think Freud would enjoy it. I have four sisters, and I remember a moment when I was running down a hall in my house without my diaper on, and dropping turds along the way. My sisters were all screaming. But I don't remember an awareness of visual form-making that was momentous. I got into movie-making when I was in the eighth grade. I was very interested in experimental film. I spent a lot of time in Chicago going to the Art Institute. And I spent my lunch hours in school reading about conceptual art in the library. This was my milieu. Sports were not, and math was not—art is what I claimed as my territory.

And how did your parents feel about that?

They were really supportive. I think they were really happy that I had found an area that I was absolutely dedicated to. I found it amazing that they were so permissive, allowing me to move to New York. When I got mugged—

You got mugged when you first came to New York?

Yes. I was like a hayseed when I first moved to New York! I looked young—I *was* young. Moving from Indiana to go to Cooper Union was a radical thing. I was very lucky that I got accepted to Cooper Union, because it was free, and I couldn't afford to go to many other schools.

It seems that your education at Cooper Union had
a profound impact on your work and the way that
you think.

It did. It amazes me when I look back over the various aspects of my career and my daily life, I can trace so much back to my coming to New York and going to Cooper Union. It was very heady and exciting and a spectacular collision of people and context

HOW TO THINK LIKE A GREAT GRAPHIC DESIGNER

and influences. And it still is. My experience at Cooper Union has influenced a lot of my intellectual heritage, the language that I use, and the values that I have about design.

How confident are you in your own judgment?

First and foremost, I believe you must have a strong idea about your work. **For me, the interesting part of design is feeling confident about the content and the approach, and then struggling with form.**

After all of the conceptualization, then you create form, and form is very unpredictable. I think that form is motivated, or rationalized, in a lot of my work and that the design is fairly intellectual. Essentially, I'm confident in my work when I feel that it is defendable, when I'm happy with the rationale, and when I can articulate it. Again, this very much comes out of my experience at Cooper Union.

Do you ever allow yourself to go straight into form if you are not confident with the approach, or with the hope that the approach will work itself out as you struggle through the form?

Yes, but it can be sloppy. It's easy to get sidetracked by form. In a way, you can say that this is the pleasure of visual thinking. I think this is what people do when they sketch a lot, which I don't do. They think through form and have the form evolve into a conceptual thought. I tend to be more abstract. I go through ideas in my mind; I don't write them down. This can be a bit ruthless, because before anything ever hits paper, it has been turned over in my mind. But if I were a designer that started with form first, the breadth of my work would look more similar. I really value my work looking different because it is about different things. So it's not led by form.

I think that a lot of Paula Scher's work can be identified as Paula's. It is very much a signature. If

I see work in a lineup, I can usually identify Paula's. But, again, the idea that design starts with form is an intrinsic part of the way that I was taught.

However, there is often a twin dichotomy that exists in really great work, when there exists a great idea that's also beautifully executed. Ideally, though, you shouldn't be able to pull something apart and say, "Well, that was a good idea, but it's ugly," or, "That's really beautiful, but there is no idea here."

How and why did you decide to become a designer?

I saw that it was a way into the world for me, and I'm not sure exactly why or how. I am very aware of environment. When I was growing up, we were always moving from one house to another, and my mother was always transforming a space physically into something else. She wasn't an interior designer, but she was very ambitious.

I remember an image of her with a sledgehammer as she took the sledgehammer to the wall of the house because she wanted the window to be bigger. She had this idea that there was a good view outside, and the window was too small. She didn't hire a contractor or a window maker, she simply decided that we were missing a good view and took the matter into her own hands.

I think that conscious remaking of our environment was profound. She didn't think of herself as a designer or an artist—she believed that if you didn't like a color, then you repaint the wall, and if you need a bigger window, than you just make your window bigger. She was a talented seamstress and a creative person, and I think this had a lot of impact on me.

How important would you say politics is to your work, or in your work?

In my earlier projects, for example, the study of the history of the kitchen and bathroom that Ellen [Lupton] and I did many years ago, the politics may have been more legible. The work included implicit critical themes about consumerism and about the role of design in manipulating people. There was also an implicit critique in a lot of my earlier writing about advertising and design.

But I have never done work that was "straight-on protest." I never did protest graphics. My work has been more engaged politically by the direction of and the nature of the critique. Lately, I haven't been doing work that allows for that, or where it's even a dimension of the project. I think when you work more commercially for clients, or on behalf of clients, your role and your message take a back seat to theirs.

Right now, I'm doing a lot of work with the Ford Foundation. It definitely has a political context, but what I'm doing for them is not political in nature. It's more supportive of philanthropy. I relate it to the famous Jean-Luc Godard quote: "I'm not interested in making political films, but in making films politically." I love that distinction. I feel like you can approach work in two ways. You can be politically straight-on, agitating for a cause, or you can engage in the process in a political way, which means challenging the system.

I feel that repositioning a designer as someone who is an author or contributor in quite a lot of the work that I do—in exhibition design or in publishing—is a political gesture. It is not everyday politics; it's more about expanding the definition of design and the role of the designer.

What do you think the role of design is in manipulating people?

It can be very significant. I think a lot of that discussion has gotten buried because of the general euphoria around design, and I don't know if we are in a moment here where it almost feels old-fashioned to critique the role of design in the manipulation of people. It's almost come full circle where people think that it's actually not manipulation, but simply giving people what they want. I feel like in some ways we are in a "post-manipulation" design environment.

Why do you think we're now experiencing a general euphoria about design?

It seems as if there is a connection now between personal fulfillment and consumer choice. I first heard this phrase "personal fulfillment" 15 to 20 years ago, and when I heard it, I felt it had a ring of soullessness. It was almost facetious. Yet it seems like that's the world we live in now. It's ironic what we have come full circle to become. I think that a lot of the contemporary ideas of "personal fulfillment" are synonymous with buying power.

Remember when having an answering machine seemed hedonistic and kind of gross?

Exactly. I know that my kids don't know what that's like. They don't have the same benchmarks.

As you get older, you get more comfortable with these accoutrements of lifestyle. Now I'm less critical about it. When you have a family, you naturally acquire more goods. I remember when Ellen and I were living in an apartment in the East Village. It was really small; but we had a different relationship to comfort, to the accumulation of goods. Now it seems rather blurry, which is a radical critique for me. Perhaps for our culture as well.

You are often referred to as both a designer and a writer, or a designer and an editor. How important is writing and editing to you in your career, and would you say that you're comfortable both as designer and writer?

Yes. It has always been important to refer to both because I think that I design like a writer and write like a designer. This came about in a more organic way than it might seem. When Ellen and I graduated from Cooper Union, it was apparent that there was incredible literature in the field of architecture. We both had the benefit of seeing it firsthand. I had taken a class at the architecture school at Cooper, and it was a legendary program headed by John Hejduk—his critiques were spectacular.

In what way were they spectacular?

People had an extreme seriousness of purpose, and it was theatrical. The architectural reviews were life and death, and the language was fascinating to hear. It was the height of pretension, with the utmost seriousness. There was an incredible quality to it. It did not compare to the level of critique and discussion that was going on in the arts school. There was a sense that the kids coming through the architecture program were dealing with issues that were shaping culture and history and had done so for thousands of years. We had to measure up, and it was incredibly compelling to watch.

And part of what we noticed in going to Cooper Union was that there was great critical literature about architecture that didn't exist in the same way in the field of graphic design. There wasn't just a lack of theory; there was also a lack of historical literature. Yes, there were some books on the history of type and there were some annuals from the Art Directors Club, or AIGA, but it wasn't a vital, intellectual history. It was a very open field. So when Ellen and I graduated from Cooper, we started writing about design. Steve Heller started his "Modernism and Eclecticism" conference, and all of a sudden, there was a growing sense of design discourse that was tremendously exciting.

The first piece I wrote was for Steve Heller, because he asked me to. Just the invitation from Steve to write something for a journal turned me into a writer. And then the experience to keep writing and continue to publish became very important to my professional identity.

Do you feel like you're better at one more than the other?

Oh, I am definitely a better designer. I know this because I do it more, and I do it more naturally. With writing, I procrastinate. I back myself into writing. Ellen is the exact opposite. She is a totally natural writer. She wakes up writing. For me, writing requires a tremendous amount of effort.

How did 2wice *magazine come to be?*

I was asked to redesign a magazine called *Dance Ink*. It was a quiet magazine that came out four times a year. It actually felt like more of a newsletter, and it did not have a strong visual identity. Redesigning it was an incredible opportunity; I wasn't given a lot of constraints. The publisher was (and still is) very interested in photography, so it was a great opportunity for me to start working with dance and photography, and to start writing about dance, and to create a very special publication. After we were nominated for a National Magazine Award, the publisher felt like she wanted a bigger framework to work in.

She invited me to propose a magazine that would be about dance, art, and design, and to create something new—that's how I came up with the premise of *2wice*. The first few issues seemed more like a really beautiful academic journal, and if you look back to the early issues, it had more of an art theory/criticism vibe that gradually moved into more of a magazine that was premised around the idea of performance.

And that's what it's become, a place to perform. This means that every document that we create has to be a unique, interesting collaboration of photography, art, design, and editorial. I still commission the writing; I edit the text, and I design the entire thing. For me, it's a laboratory of design, writing, and research coming together into one compelling object. I am very proud of it.

Do you ever feel insecure as a designer? Do you ever
feel insecure about your work?

Sure. I think that's an ongoing struggle. I want to
stay relevant, and not fall into a rut. I think that
my prevailing concern is worrying if I'm doing too
much of the same thing: Am I too concerned with
conventional notions of beauty and good taste? But
if it's not that, I'm thinking about whether or not
something is too edgy.

**What interests me in architecture and
design is work that is awkward, and not beautiful, and a
little bit idiosyncratic.**
I have such a love of typography that I feel like
it's catnip. I have to be careful that it doesn't seduce
me to the point that I end up resting on the beauty
of lettering.

Where do you see yourself in five years?

Well, I'd love to be able to work in a number of
different areas. Last year, I designed wallpaper for
Knoll, and it was really interesting, as the end product wasn't a book or an exhibition. It was something
that was designed and then traveled into another
territory, and it became a material that other designers might use. I'd love to do more of that.

I definitely want to continue the exhibition
work that I'm doing, but I also love the more mod-
est scale of product design. And I have been slowly
ratcheting up the ambition of the photography that
I'm art-directing, and I'd love to do much more
ambitious work with photography, either as an
art director or as a photographer. If I take the next
step, it might be to actually figure out how to be the
photographer. I spend a lot of time art-directing
photography, and I often wonder what the work
would look like if I photographed it myself.

Do you consider yourself to be an ambitious person?

I don't think of myself in that way, but when I think

how much I take on, I realize I must be. The image
I have of myself is that I'm just a nice, unassuming,
"aw shucks" kind of person. But then I wonder if I
am indeed that way, then why am I hungering for
the next thing? I also think that designers require
this insatiable quality to be successful in design and
to keep things interesting.

So you are always looking for new things?

Yes. I am restless. I think that restlessness and ambition go hand in hand. Things aren't quite enough,
or they are never quite right, or never quite finished,
or they could be better.

How do you know when something is finished?

When the time comes that you have just got to put it
away. For me, that's usually the big motivating force.
I would say that if there weren't deadlines for things
that had to go to press, they would just sit around
and get mulled over and finessed for ages. It's painful for me to say, "Okay, it's really got to go now."

What do you like best about being a designer?

Design is a way into learning about, supporting,
improving, and magnifying the world. You can
assemble a worldview based on the clients that
you take on and the subjects you work with. For
me, design is about art, architecture, fashion, and
performance.

Design is an unusual field. It has depths of
engagement. And in any area I'm working in, I'm
striving toward making something more under-
standable, more accessible, and more beautiful.
As I'm engaging with all of these subjects, I'm
constantly learning about them and being influenced by them, and that is amazing. Truly amazing.

Massimo Vignelli

Massimo Vignelli was one of the few designers I had not personally met prior to our interview, and as a result, I nervously anticipated our conversation. It didn't help that I inadvertently stood up Massimo for our first scheduled interview. I mistakenly scribbled down our appointment in the wrong date on my calendar and missed the meeting entirely— not realizing until many hours later that I had kept Massimo waiting. Fortunately for me, he took it in stride, even graciously suggesting that it was better that we hadn't met that day, since, while he was waiting for me to arrive, something had come up that he needed to resolve.

This alone highlights Massimo's incredible spirit, his joie de vivre, his humor, and his generosity. Universally considered one of the great design artisans of our time, Massimo is also a quintessential gentleman. Not satisfied with anything less than elegant, he is erudite, charming, and cute, even. Yes, I said it: Massimo Vignelli is cute.

When he left a message alerting me of our missed rendezvous, he reassured me it was quite all right and requested that we reschedule. Despite my nerves, our subsequent meeting was delightful, and he shared with me thoughts on love, his wife and partner Leila Vignelli, his penchant for the color black, and the friendship he had with Alan Fletcher.

How important, if at all, is writing to your work?

> Well, I write all the time. Of course, my English is limited and my writing follows my English. But somehow the writing is better; at least there is less of an accent! I am a maniac about being semantically correct. I find that when I write, I automatically look for the perfect word more often than I do when I speak. I want to have the exact word that says exactly what I mean as precisely as possible.

Why did you choose to live in New York?

> It's a long story. The quick answer is that we started the company with some friends here in the U.S., and we opened an office in New York. The person who was supposed to run the office got sick. I was in Milan at the time and I was commuting back and forth. I got tired of flying over twice a month, and so we [Vignelli and his wife, Leila] decided to come over and run the office for a while and then go back. We're still here after 40 years.
>
> [*Laughter.*]
>
> We're still here. New York is a fabulous city. It's like a magnet. I can't leave anymore. There is nothing that can compare to New York. And it is not even beautiful. There are hundreds, thousands of other cities that are much more beautiful. But there is only one New York.

What do you think contributes to making it so special?

> It's the energy. It's the way people walk, it's the way people talk. It's the way people live. You know: In New York, people dress in black all the time.

Why do you think so many people wear black in New York?

> Because of the image.

How would you describe it?

> To begin with, black has class. It's the best color.

There is no other color that is better than black. There are many others that are appropriate and happy, but those colors belong on flowers. Black is a color that is man-made. It is really a projection of the brain. It is a mind color. It is intangible. It is practical. It works 24 hours a day. In the morning or afternoon, you can dress in tweed, but in the evening, you look like a professor who escaped from college. Everything else has connotations that are different, but black is good for everything. My house is covered in black.

Are all your clothes black? Do you wear all black?
Yes. Always. Always.

So when did you make the decision that you wanted to be a designer?
When I was 14 years old, extremely early in my life.

What happened?
I went to a house of a friend of mine, and his mother had just finished redecorating. And all of sudden, I discovered that somebody was responsible for doing these kinds of things. Nothing happened by itself. That fascinated me. I went home and started to design. I read books and magazines about these things so I became more educated. And I got more and more involved, so that by the time I was 18, I knew exactly what I wanted to do.

Have you always been so driven?
Yes. It's amazing, I have tremendous passion. Tremendous. Curiosity and passion. My passion is bigger, but my curiosity is equally as strong.

You never had any aspirations to do anything else? It was always to be a designer?
Exactly. I never thought of doing anything else. Not once in my life. Every book that I was reading,

every preference was devoted to architecture and design. No technology or philosophy books. Very few novels. I don't have a literal mind.

How would you describe your mind?

It is visual.

What do you think is the difference between a literary mind and a visual mind?

A visual mind is interested in anything that you see, and a literary mind is interested in anything you think. A literary mind is interested in people. A visual mind is interested in things, objects, nature. This doesn't mean that you look and don't think. Of course, you do that, too. But a literary mind is more prone to thinking than looking visually. These type of people like to read. They like to analyze things from a psychological point of view. Writers like this write about isolation, and some write about being together. Each one investigates one action of the mind. And the mind, being as complex as it is, is an endless source of investigation.

Do you feel your work is immediately identifiable as your work? Do you feel you have a style?

Yes and no. After many years of exposure, in some ways it is. My work has a certain discipline, a rigor, and a minimalist expression. I use a very limited choice of colors: primarily black and red. To me, black is black and red is color. That's it.

And what about your preference for Bodoni?

Bodoni is one of the most elegant typefaces ever designed. When I talk about elegance, I mean intellectual elegance. Elegance of the mind.

How would you define elegance of the mind?

I would define intellectual elegance as a mind that is continually refining itself with education and knowledge. Intellectual elegance is the opposite of intellectual vulgarity. We all know vulgarity very well. Elegance is the opposite.

I have to ask: What would you consider to be vulgar?

Vulgarity is something underneath culture and education. Anything that is not refined. There are manifestations of primitive cultures or ethnic cultures that could be extremely refined and elegant, but don't belong to our kind of refinery or culture. Culture is the accumulation of at least 10,000 years. You can really say that intellectual elegance is the by-product of refinement. One of the greatest things about vulgarity is that it tends to continuously disappear.

My friend Umberto Eco wrote a book about beauty, and now he's writing a book about ugliness. He told me the last time I saw him that it was much more difficult to write a book about ugliness than to write one about beauty. It's the same with vulgarity, in a sense.

What do you think design is really about?

Number one, design is a profession that takes care of everything around us. Politicians take care of the nation and fix things—at least they are supposed to. Architects take care of buildings. Designers take care of everything around us. Everything that is around us—this table, this chair, this lamp, this pen—has been designed. All of these things, every-thing has been designed by somebody.

I think that it is my responsibility to make the work better than it is. That is my number one prior-ity. The second priority is to decrease the amount of vulgarity by replacing the vulgarity with things that are more refined.

When we work with clients, we make it quite clear from the beginning that we don't intend to create vulgar things. Most of the time, we don't even have to say this; when a client comes in, they know what we are doing, and they want us to do things for them in this way. So we don't have too much to fight over! But even in the client discussions, they can see that this is what we want to do.

So what is design all about? It is to decrease the amount of vulgarity in the world. It is to make the world a better place to be. But everything is relative. There is a certain amount of latitude between what is good, what is elegant, and what is refined that can take many, many manifestations. It doesn't have to be one style. We're not talking about style, we're talking about quality. Style is tangible, quality is intangible. I am talking about creating for everything that surrounds us a level of quality.

You use the word elegance in contrast to vulgarity. Where does beauty fit in this?

On the elegant side.

Do you feel that they're intertwined?

Absolutely. They are simultaneous. There is no beauty in vulgarity. There can be fascination in vulgarity, but there is no beauty. A vulgar woman is never beautiful.

Do you think there are equal amounts of fascination in vulgarity and beauty?

I'm not fascinated by vulgarity, but some people certainly are. A lot of people are. Take the phenomenon of Las Vegas. It's fascinating, but the fascination is its vulgarity. Nevertheless, it's fascinating. I swore that I would never go to Las Vegas, and when I went, I never wanted to leave.

Why do you think people are fascinated by vulgarity?

Because it is easier to absorb. Elegance is about education and refinement, and it is a by-product of a continual search for the best and for the sublime.

And it is a continuous refusal of indulging in anything that is vulgar. It's a job.

How do you know when you've created something that's good?

It sparkles. It has a ring by itself.

A ring by itself?

When you start working on something, you are aiming for a specific target. You have the target in your mind and a bull's-eye. And I try to aim at that bull's-eye. If you hit it, you're very happy. And that's when you know that you've finished, that you've found the solution to the problem.

Do you ever have situations where you love something and your client doesn't?

No. Because whatever we do answers a particular set of circumstances that is known to the client. You can see the answer right there. That's why it's called "the solution of a problem" in our jargon. The client comes with a problem, which is the same way we go to a doctor with a problem. The doctor analyzes you and gives you a diagnosis of the situation and then a cure to make you better. We do the same thing. We try to eliminate everything that is wrong in the same way a doctor does. He can see the symptoms of your disease. That's what we do. We see the symptoms of the client's disease, and we correct it. We keep what is good and throw away what is wrong.

How do you feel about companies or clients that insist upon doing a lot of market research?

I let them go.

You let them go? You don't work with them at all?

I never work with middle management. Middle managers are dominated by the fear of losing their jobs, and therefore they have no sense of risk. I always work with the top person—the president or the owner of a company. That's it. Only the person at the top can take risk. He's used to it. That is how he got to the position he's in. He understands what you are doing, and he doesn't have to report to anybody. He makes his decision, and that's the way it goes. I don't believe in market research. I don't believe in marketing the way it's done in America. The American way of marketing is to answer to the wants of the customer instead of answering to the needs of the customer. The purpose of marketing should be to find needs—not to find wants.

People do not know what they want. They barely know what they need, but they definitely do not know what they want. They're conditioned by the limited imagination of what is possible. But very often, when focus groups are conducted, marketers listen to ten people who say they don't like something, and then they don't do it. If five people out of ten say they don't like, they don't do it. The "researchers" never probe beyond why the people don't like what they don't like. This just builds a platform of ignorance. Most of the time, focus groups are built on the pressure of ignorance.

Doctors do not operate this way. They do not conduct a focus group to see if you have cancer or not.

Have you ever been afraid of failing?
No.

No? You aren't afraid of anything?
Vulgarity taking over. **My life is a continual struggle, a continuous battle against vulgarity taking over.**

Were you ever interested in being an artist?
No. I am a natural-born designer.

How do you generally start a project?

By listening as much as I can. I am convinced the solution is always in the problem. You could do a design that you like, but it doesn't solve the problem. Design must solve a problem. Then, the design is exciting. But I find it extremely difficult. This is why I respect artists. Without a problem, I don't exist. Artists are lucky; they can work by themselves. They don't need a problem.

How much collaboration do you have with Leila on your projects?

Sometimes we work on a specific project together. She has a very good, critical mind. As we say, "I propose, she disposes." I'm the one who usually comes up with the initial ideas, and she's the one who evaluates which is the best one. She determines if it's the right or the wrong approach. If it's the wrong approach, we'll talk about which one is the right one and why. She also does many projects on her own.

Do you ever argue?

All the time. One hundred percent of the time.

Would you say she's your muse?

No.

Do you have a muse?

That depends. Sometimes. But Leila is not a muse, no. She's a critic.

How would you define love?

That's a good question. Let's see if I can define it. I haven't been asked this in a while. I would say there are several layers. Love is a cake that comes in layers. The top layer is the most appealing one. This is the one you see first. Then you cut into it and you see many different layers. They're all beautiful, but some are sweeter than others.

How do I define love? I define it as a very intense passion on the one hand, and a very steady level on the other. The first layer, the one of passion, is the most troublesome. God, it's a pain.

Why?

Because the more you love, the more jealous you get. You become jealous of everything, the air around the person, the people, a look, even the way they look at something. Then there is the extreme pleasure of writing about love, as well. This is fascinating to me. The layer of correspondence—and the anxiety to receive answers. That is great.

Finally you come to the physical layer. The emotion of receiving and conveying pleasure is sensational. It's unbelievable how your entire body becomes a messenger. Your fingers, lips, eyes, smells. Your whole body becomes involved.

Then there is the layer of suffering. Distance, remoteness, no presence, horror. The suffering of not seeing who you want to see, and not being with whom you love. This is another painful aspect of love. We are talking about pain. All these layers define love. I think that is why it's so great and so extremely complex.

Have you been in love many times?

Well, in life these things happen.

When was the last time you cried?

Over the death of a good friend. It was a very short time ago.

[*Stops speaking.*]

I am sorry, I can't talk about it.

[*Starts crying.*]

Massimo, I'm so sorry.

That's okay. Did you know Alan Fletcher? A great, great designer. So you have your answer. I cry about the loss of someone who could have continuously made a great contribution.

Do you think that there's a common denominator to people who can make a great contribution? Do you think that there's something that—

Unites them? Yes. What in Greek is called sympathy, the synchronization of pathos. You feel this incredible level of connection with these people. To a certain extent, it is equally comparable to love.

When are you happiest?

When something that I work on comes out well. That's one. When I work with somebody who I love. That's another. It doesn't have to be a big love. It could be a minor one.

[*Laughter.*]

It's like pain. I keep going back to this analogy with pain. There are pains that are major, pains that are minor. And there's not just one pain during life. Pains come and go.

When was the last time you got really angry?

I get angry when something is done wrong when it could have been done right. Work-related things make me mad, if something has been done wrong: wrong colors, wrong type, wrong paper, wrong material, whatever it is—if it's wrong.

What's your best quality?

I don't even know if I have any. Nothing. Which one of them do I have?

What about your worst? What is your worst one?

My worst one? Ego.

You have a big ego?

Yes, I have a big ego.

[*Laughter.*]

Have you ever been in analysis or therapy?

No. No. I am happy. I don't have psychological traumas to overcome. One of the great advantages of being so concentrated on your work is that it is all there is. Everything I do comes into this and enriches me. Everything, even every book I read, enriches me.

Who do you feel is doing good work right now?

A good designer that I respect is Milton [Glaser]. I really like his way of thinking. He's extremely talented. Brilliant mind, terrific mind. And of course, my Michael. Michael Bierut. My favorite designer right now is in Germany. His name is Pierre Mendell. Look for his work. He is a great one. He has such a great ability to synthesize. You were asking what I admire: **I am interested in "essence"—my major aim is really to get to the essence of the problem, and just throw away everything that's not pertinent to it.** At the end of a project, my work should be the projection of that experience, the essence of effect. It's a habit that you get into.

How do you get to the essence?

The essence is what is left when there's nothing else that you can throw away.

Is there anything that you haven't done that you want to do?

Oversee the redesign of the Vatican. Such a joke! Can you imagine? The pope as a client! That'd be lovely, turning to the pope and saying, "Well, the symbol is okay. We can live with that, but everything else has to go."

Acknowledgments

How to Think Like a Great Graphic Designer *took both a year and a lifetime to write. Many people, near and far, helped make this book possible, and it is my sincere honor to acknowledge their contribution. First and foremost, my eternal gratitude to Steven Heller for recommending me to Allworth Press, and sincere appreciation to Tad Crawford and Nicole Potter-Talling for actually taking his recommendation seriously. I am additionally grateful to Nicole for answering my overwhelming number of questions with kindness, speed, and patience; and to Allison Caplin for her grace under pressure and keen eye.*

I am grateful to Simon Williams, my dear partner at Sterling Brands, for all of his support, encouragement, and trust. Sterling is a special place, and I must thank Elliott Calo, Gregory St. John, Clara Hendon, Jen Simon, and, especially, Lisa Grant for everything that they do, every day.

Huge gratitude to the kind and generous people who supported me on the journey toward this book in vast and innumerable ways: Jenny Fenig and Kim Rivielle, Brian Travis, the entire staff at Print *magazine (past and present), the authors of* Speak Up, *Alissa Walker, Bryn Mooth, Ric Grefé and the National and New York Chapters of AIGA, the professional association of design, Richard Wilde and the School of Visual Arts in New York, and my friends at Adobe: Courtney Spain, Joan Bodensteiner, and Ashwini Jamboktar.*

My life would not be the same without the love and inspiration that I receive from the remarkable people I am lucky to call friends and family: Marian Bantjes, Pamela DeCesare, Cheryl & Craig Swanson, Armin Vit & Bryony Gomez-Palacio, Simon Lince & Cary Leibowitz, Lisa Francella & Louise Carravone, Sandra Kiersky, John Fulbrook III & Catharine Wragg, Barbara deWilde, Mark Kingsley, Lisa Rousseau, Margie Butler, Marcus & Susan Hewitt, the Feinman family: Lewis, Judith, Ilene, Michael, Cathy, Kenny, Ben, Maia, Jessica, Rebecca, and Erica, Maria Anthis, Alan & Beth Dye, Laura Victore, Brian Rea, Amy Dresner, Felix Sockwell, Amanda Bach, Andrea Dezsö, Bill Grant, William & Irma Lunderman, Darralyn Reith, Christine Mau, Jan Winarsky & Kayla Green, Alexandra Alcantara, Ethan Trask, Josh Liberson, Peter Buchanan-Smith, Jay Gould, Christine & Joe Melchione, Steve Ginsberg, Pamela Parisi, Marianne Klimchuk, and Noreen Morioka & Sean Adams.

Special, heartfelt thanks to my four lifelong best friends, Susan Benjamin, Katharine Umsted, Susan Milligan, and Megan Taylor: Thank you for always being there and for always giving so unconditionally.

To my father, Martin Millman, my stepmom Georganna Millman, and to my brothers, Josh and Jake: You mean everything to me; my life would not be the same without your grace and love.

And to those who helped me create this book: to all of the extraordinary designers featured in these pages, and to Edwin Rivera, Jason Ramirez, Jürgen Miller, Joyce Rutter Kaye, Grant McCracken, Malcolm Gladwell, and Steven Heller (again), I will always be indebted to you.

And to my talented co-conspirators, Rodrigo Corral and Jeremy Lehrer, quite simply: I could not have done this without you. Thank you from the bottom of my heart.

About the Author

Debbie Millman has worked in the design business for over two decades. She is a managing partner and president of the design division at Sterling Brands, one of the country's leading brand consultancies. As host of the Internet talk show "Design Matters," the popular forum for commentary and conversation on visual culture, Millman has established herself as one of design journalism's leaders. She is on the national board of the AIGA and writes for the design blog Speak Up. An instructor at the School of Visual Arts and a regular contributor to Print *magazine, she lives in New York City.*

Index

A

abundance, 33
accomplishment, 50
acting, 147–148
advertising, 63, 72, 74, 90–91
age, 20, 176
AIGA (America Institute
of Graphic Arts), 103, 209
Alfred A. Knopf, 135, 137
Allgemeine Gewerbeschule,
185
ambition, 176, 206, 211–212
American Institute of
Graphic Arts (AIGA), 183
anger, 13, 55–56, 223
apprenticeship, 106
approval, 6, 43, 44
architecture, 146, 208–209,
211
Arena magazine, 75–76
art
advertising v., 74
conceptual, 204
elitist world of, 69
experience, 53
graphic design v., 57–59,
68, 80–81, 83, 90, 177–
178
work and, 29
Art Commission of New York,
43–44
Atlantic Records, 41
audience, 2, 100, 177, 185, 194,
201. *See also* clients
authenticity, 3
awards, 163

B

Bacon, Paul, 106
Balkind, Aubrey, 170
Bass, Saul, 62, 83
Batman Collected (Kidd), 135
beauty, 27, 218
Below the Fold (Helfand), 150
Bernard, Pierre, 107
Biber, Jim, 23
Bierut, Michael, xi, 5–17, 26,
169, 170, 192, 224
black, 214–215
blogs, x, 149–150
Bodoni, 216
books, 144
brain, 45–46, 97, 102, 165, 215
Brand New, 198
branding, x, 62–63
Brody, Neville, 67–76
business, 175
Byrne, David, 191, 193

C

calendar, 10–11
Carin Goldberg Design, 19
Cassandre, A. M., 187
Catalog (Goldberg), 19
CBS Records, 22, 41
celebrity, 69–71, 145
cell phones, 154
Cheese Monkeys, The
(Kidd), 135
Chermayeff & Geismar, 183
Chip Kidd: Book One: Work:
1986–2006 (Kidd), 135
Christmas Carol, A
(Dickens), 109

Chwast, Seymour, 155–159
clients, 58–59, 73, 79, 100, 107,
129, 185, 200–201, 207,
217–218, 219
anger at, 55
chemistry with, 186
presenting work to,
166–167, 176–177
satisfaction of, 179
working with, 47–48
collaboration, 137
Colors magazine, 93
comics, 126
commercialism, 69, 72
communication, 69, 78–79, 83,
88–89, 92, 177
community, 40
compromise, 22, 95–96, 107
compulsion, 13–14
computers, hands v., 110, 117,
137, 148, 181, 185, 198
confidence, 123
connections, 171
consciousness, 33, 40
consumerism, 63–64, 207
content
of graphic design, 24–25,
205–206
sexual, 143
style v., 153
contentment, creativity v.,
142
conviction, 6
Cooper Union School of Art,
156, 194, 200, 204–205
creativity, 14–17, 174, 193, 199,
201

contentment v., 142
  destruction and, 31
  freedom and, 107
  miracles and, 30
critical literature, 5, 209
criticism, 122, 207, 209, 221
crossword puzzles, 139
culture, 121–122, 157–158,
    165–166, 217
  American, 89, 208
  generic, 71
  matriarchal, 169
  pop, 78–80, 81, 91
curiosity, 215

D

Dance Ink magazine, 210
de Bono, Edward, 61
deadlines, 48–49, 119, 174, 212
death, 54–55
design. See graphic design
"Design Matters," ix
Design Observer, 5, 8, 145, 149
Design Writing Research
    (Miller), 203
designers. See graphic
    designers
Designism, 39
devotion, 38
dharma, 104, 113
Dickens, Charles, 109
disagreements, 95
Disney, Walt, 156
distraction, 10
Doyle, Stephen, 191–201
drama, 38
drawing, 30, 68, 126, 128,
    139–140, 148, 163, 166, 185
dreams, 141, 152–153
Drenttel, William, 152
Duniho, Pat, 110

E

Eco, Umberto, 217
education, 83, 128, 136–137,
    140, 151, 157, 162–163,
    197–198, 216
elders, 86
elegance, 216–217, 218
environment, 206
essence, 224

F

Face, The, magazine, 67, 74–75
Factory Records, 82, 88
fame, 57–58
fashion, 36, 80, 87, 91
fear, 101, 113, 142, 158, 220
  love v., 34
  no, 197–198
  making the right decision
    despite, 23
Fella, Ed, 54
Fetish magazine, 67
"Fighter," 122
Fili, Louise, 23
First Things First manifesto,
    153–154, 188
First Things First 2000,
    143, 188
Fletcher, Alan, 222–223
flounder, 21
4AD, 175–176
freedom, 107, 118
Freud, Sigmund, 204
friendship, 120
From Lascaux to Brooklyn,
    120
fun, 26
Futura, 89

G

Garland, Ken, 143, 188
Gebrausgraphik magazine,
    156
Geissbuhler, Steff, 2, 183–189
Gelman, Alexander, 130
Gilbert, Danny, 56
Glaser, Milton, 3, 22, 29–40,
    83, 143, 178, 189, 193, 200,
    224
goals, 168, 219
God, 108
Godard, Jean-Luc, 207
Goldberg, Carin, 19–28
Golden, William, 146
graphic design, 2–3, 63–64,
    194, 211, 212, 220. *See also*
    record covers; work
  accomplishments of,
    49–50
  art v., 57–59, 68, 80–81, 83,
    90, 177–178
  assessing, 121

business, 23, 87
cinema v., 56
communication of, 78–79,
    84, 89, 177
content in, 24–25,
    205–206
creativity and, 14–15
cult pop, 78–80
decoration v., 91
definition of, 43, 59, 137,
    147–148, 156, 178, 207
dynamic, 130–131
education, 83
effects of, 39, 85
evolution of, 23–24, 49,
    87–88
good v. bad, 7, 120
as interface, 91
love of, 181
manipulation in, 207–208
paradigms of, 46–47
radical, 72
science v., 200
self-expression v., 128–130
style, 25, 49, 153, 164, 218
truth and, 90–91
youth-oriented business
    of, 20
graphic designers, 20, 39, 92,
    139
  celebrity status of, 70–71
  collaboration with, 137
  problems for, 3, 15, 91, 220
  responsibility of, 70, 82,
    131, 144, 159, 217
  role of, 207
  self-taught, 140
*Graphic Language of Neville
    Brody, The* (Brody), 67
Gray, Cleve, 151

H

habits, 7
happiness, 32, 56, 119
Harmon, Marshall, 171–172
Harvard University, 56
Hayman, Luke, 12
Heartfield, John, 132
Hejduk, John, 209
Helfand, Jessica, 145–154
Heller, Steve, 209
Helvetica, 89, 123, 188

HOW TO THINK LIKE A GREAT GRAPHIC DESIGNER

High Street, 88
Hofmann, Armin, 187–188
humanity, 3, 195
humor, 197
Hunter, Kent, 15

I
identity, 40
ignorance, 220
illustration, 42, 157
imagination, 16, 177, 192, 199, 220
imitation, 75
insecurity, 37, 98, 211
"Inside the Actors Studio," ix
Institute for Architecture and Urban Studies, The, 146
Internet, 109
interviews, job, 169–171, 178
invention, 46, 60, 76
IRS, 13

J
jealousy, 221–222
journal, 140, 150
Joyce, James, 24
Julius Caesar, 193

K
Kalman, Tibor, 9, 19, 23, 54, 73, 93, 109, 191
karma, 57
Kauffer, E. McKnight, 24
Kemp, David, 171–172
Kent State, 127
Kidd, Chip, 135–144
kids, 121
King, Carole, 22
Kirby, Jack, 133
knowledge, 128
Koons, Jeff, 81

L
language, 74, 164, 194, 195
learning, 32–33, 194. *See also* education
lifestyle, 34–35, 208
Lionni, Leo, 101
Lipton, James, ix
lists, 112–113
literature, critical, 5, 209

Little Blue and Little Yellow (Lionni), 100–101
logic, 199
logos, 167
Lolita, 143
Looking Closer: Critical Writings on Graphic Design, 5
love, 221–222
fear v., 34
of graphic design, 181
money v., 118
Lubalin, Herb, 116
Lucky magazine, 93
Lupton, Ellen, 171, 203, 206, 209, 210
Lust for Life, 64

M
M&Co, 93
"Mad as Hell," 103
Madonna, 19
Maeda, John, 115–123
magazines, 37, 67, 93, 191, 201, 210. *See also* specific types
The Man Who Mistook His Wife for a Hat (Sacks), 24
manifesto, 26, 143, 153, 154, 188
manipulation, 207–208
Marcos, Ferdinand, 162
marketing, 219–220
Mau, Bruce, 2
"Maximus, to himself," 35
McCoy, Kathy, 170
Meat Loaf, 173
media, radical, 71
mediocrity, 71
memory, 31–32
men, 78, 96–97
Mendell, Pierre, 224
military, 104
Miller, Abbott, 26, 203–212
Millman, Debbie, ix
mind, visual v. literary, 216. *See also* brain
miracles, 30
MIT, 115
Modern English, 179
"Modernism and Eclecticism," 209

money, 32, 36, 44, 91, 108, 109, 118, 188
Moody, Rick, 125
Morandi, Giorgio, 38
Murdoch, Iris, 34
music business, 54, 84, 175, 177, 180. *See also* record covers
My Name is Asher Lev, 104

N
narcissism, 34–35
networking, 170–171, 176
New Order, 84–85
New York, 41, 43–44, 55, 106, 169, 204, 214
New York Post, The, 141
New York School, The, 89
New York Times, The, 107, 141, 144, 197
New Yorker, 57
notebook, 11–12. *See also* journal; sketchbooks
"Nothing But Flowers," 9
Number 17, 93, 95

O
Oberman, Emily, 93–102, 105
obsession, 13, 78, 132
Odgers, Jayme, 131–132
Oliver, Vaughan, 173–181
Olson, Charles, 35
O.O.P.S., 125
opportunity, 21

P
pain, 222, 223
Pamuk, Orhan, 138
"Paradise by the Dashboard Light," 173
Parsons School of Design, 156
partnership, 94–96, 97, 186
Partridge, Chris, 136
"The Passenger," 64–66
passion, 215, 221
past, 31
Penn State, 136, 140
Pentagram, 12, 41, 83, 86–88, 89–90
people, 9, 89, 122, 167, 168, 174
perception, 121
perfection, 198

performativity, 2
personal fulfillment, 208
Philippines, 169
photography, 211
Pinocchio, 156
planning, 43
politics, 206–207
Pop, Iggy, 64–66
postmodernism, 23
"Power, Corruption, & Lies," 85
problems, 3, 15, 91, 220
product, quality v. branding of, 63
punk rock, 81, 175, 179
purpose, 168
Push Pin Studios, 155
pyramid structure, 87

Q
QuarkXPress, 139
questions, asking, 106

R
Rand, Paul, xi, 62, 87, 107, 118, 120, 121, 145
reading, 10, 121
record covers, 79, 82, 92, 177, 179
Reed, Lou, 56, 58
regret, 98
rejection, 159
relationships, 97
research, 121, 138, 158, 185, 203
    historical, 149
    market, 219
right action, fear v., 23
right to thought, 72
risk, 219
rock star, 57–58

S
Sacks, Oliver, 24
Sadek, George, 199, 200
Sagmeister, Stefan, 9, 53–66, 70, 73
Sahre, Paul, 95, 125–133
Saturn, 167
Saville, Peter, 77–92, 140
scarcity, 33
Scher, Paula, 6, 19, 23, 24, 27, 41–51, 205
schtick, 20–21

Schulz, Charles, 126, 142–143
scrapbook, 140
security, 34, 37
self-doubt, 174, 180
self-expression, 90, 128–130
shock value, 71
Siegler, Bonnie, 93–102
sketchbooks, 150, 185
sketching, 14, 185, 188
Snow White, 156
social change, 144, 153–154, 218
society, 39, 70–71, 74
solutions, 2, 197, 219, 220
Speak Up, x
Spy magazine, 201
staff-to-student ratio, 180
Steinberg, Saul, 107
Stewart, Martha, 198–199
studio, small v. big, 61–62
style, graphic design, 25, 49, 153, 164, 218
success, 44, 130
survival, work v., 32–34
Sutnar, Ladislav, 151
Swatch, 24
sympathy, 222–223

T
talent, 58
Talking Heads, 9
teaching, 38–39, 120
technology
    humanization of, 115
    keeping up with, 175
Tenazas, Lucille, 161–172
text, 123. *See also* typography
Tharp, Twyla, 109
"Things I've Learned in My Life So Far," 56–57
thinking, 38, 197
Thompson, Bradbury, 151
time, 119, 145. *See also* deadlines
"Time Waits For No Fan," 145
Towey, Gael, 191, 196
truth, 90–91, 111
"12 Steps on the Graphic Designer's Road to Hell," 33, 143, 189
23 Envelope, 173
2wice, 210

Tyler, Steven, 57
typography, 41, 43, 54, 59, 89, 120–121, 164, 187, 188, 211, 216

U
Ulysses (Joyce), 24
universe, abundance v. scarcity in, 33
Updike, John, 138

V
v23, 173
Valicenti, Rick, 15
Victore, James, 103–113
Vignelli, Massimo, 6–7, 15, 83, 169, 213–224
Vit, Armin, x, 198
vulgarity, 216–218, 220

W
Walker, Scott, 176
Walters, Barbara, x
Warhol, Andy, 101
Winterhouse, 145, 148, 150
Wolf, Henry, 200
women, men v., 96–97
word association, 105
words, 148
work, 32, 88, 91. *See also* graphic design
    alone, 117, 137
    art and, 29
    beauty in, 27
    completion of, 110, 138, 149, 157, 179, 185, 196, 212
    credit for, 144
    as cyclic, 123
    devotion to, 38
    difficult, 73
    free, 47
    free v. paid, 109
    with hands v. computers, 110, 117, 137, 148, 181, 185, 198
    happiness from, 32, 119
    intellectual v. intuitive, 165
    leaving behind, 133
    meaning of, 92
    mediocre, 59–60

HOW TO THINK LIKE A GREAT GRAPHIC DESIGNER

for money v. god, 108
for money v. love, 118
motivation of, 36, 112,
    129–130
open-ended, 72–73
presenting, 166–167,
    176–177
process, 14, 20, 45, 46, 61,
    131, 138, 148, 156–157,
    165–166, 176–177, 185,
    201
repetition of, 9–10, 60
self-evaluation of, 35,
    46–47, 108, 119,
    138–139, 149, 186
subconscious, 8, 46
successful, 130
survival v., 32–34
talking about v. doing, 143
timeless, 180
turning down, 195
whittling, 111
world, caring for, 39
writing, 139, 186, 208–210, 214

Y

Yale, 147–148, 151
youth, 20, 78

Z

zone, the 131–132

Books from Allworth Press

Allworth Press is an imprint of Skyhorse Publishing, Inc. Selected titles are listed below.

Brand Thinking and Other Noble Pursuits
by Debbie Millman (6 x 9, 336 pages, paperback, $19.95)

Emotional Branding: The New Paradigm for Connecting Brands to People, Updated and Revised Edition
by Marc Gobe (6 x 9, 352 pages, paperback, $19.95)

Design Thinking: Integrating Innovation, Customer Experience, and Brand Value
by Thomas Lockwood (6 x 9, 304 pages, paperback, $24.95)

Brandjam: Humanizing Brands Through Emotional Design
by Marc Gobe (6¼ x 9 ¼, 352 pages, hardcover, $24.95)

Branding the Man: Why Men Are the Next Frontier in Fashion Retail
by Bertrand Pellegrin (6 x 9, 224 pages, hardcover, $27.50)

Design Firms Open for Business
by Steven Heller and Lita Talarico (7 ⅜ x 9 ¼, 256 pages, paperback, $24.95)

Branding for Nonprofits
by D.K. Holland (6 x 9, 208 pages, paperback, $19.95)

POP: How Graphic Design Shapes Popular Culture
by Steven Heller (6 x 9, 288 pages, paperback, $24.95)

Design Disasters: Great Designers, Fabulous Failures, & Lessons Learned
edited by Steven Heller (6 x 9, 240 pages, paperback, $24.95)

Green Graphic Design
by Brian Dougherty with Celery Design Collaborative (6 x 9, 212 pages, paperback, $24.95)

Designers Don't Read
by Austin Howe; designed by Fredrik Averin (5 ½ x 8 ½, 208 pages, paperback, $19.95)

Designers Don't Have Influences
by Austin Howe (5 ½ x 8 ½, 224 pages, paperback, $19.95)

Designing Logos: The Process of Creating Symbols That Endure
by Jack Gernsheimer (8 ½ x 10, 224 pages, paperback, $35.00)

Advertising Design and Typography
by Alex W. White (8 ½ x 11, 220 pages, paperback, $50.00)

The Elements of Graphic Design, Second Edition
by Alex W. White (8 x 10, 224 pages, paperback, $29.95)

Creating the Perfect Design Brief, Second Edition: How to Manage Design for Strategic Advantage
by Peter L. Phillips (5 ½ x 8 ¼, 240 pages, paperback, $19.95)

To see our complete catalog or to order online, please visit *www.allworth.com*.